To the memory of
my sister Cynthia and my brother Grayland...
both gone too soon.

Cynthia Yvette Johnson
and
Grayland Dewayne Johnson

Published by Watersprings Media House, LLC.
P.O. Box 1284
Olive Branch, MS 38654
Contact publisher for permission requests and bulk orders.
www.waterspringsmedia.com

Printed in the United States of America.

Library of Congress Control Number: 2018934152

ISBN: 978-0-9988249-9-4

31 Days of
SONshine
Daily Devotionals, Reflections, and Prayers

Healing for the Mind,
Soul, Body, and Spirit

JANICE J. BROWNE, PH.D.

Watersprings
MEDIA HOUSE

Dedication

This book is dedicated to God my Father who placed this book in my head and heart.

To Jesus for making the opportunity possible and who is the Author and Finisher of my faith and this book.

To the Holy Spirit who inspired and guided me all the way through the writing of this beautiful and gloriously uplifting book.

To my mother, Dr. Mildred Poole Johnson a true Prayer Warrior and phenomenal lady in every way who continues to teach me from her wealth of deep wisdom and knowledge. A woman of extraordinary strength and courage who loves God without question and has led thousands to Christ through the sharing of His love for them. My favorite response to your words "I love you" is "Mother, I love you more!"

To my father, the late Elder Washington Johnson Sr., a Christian gentleman of exceptional and rare quality. He was a man of deep conviction, integrity, and love. He had a generous spirit filled with the love of God. His positive imprint is seen throughout this book and will positively imprint your life as you read it. Thank you, Heavenly Father, for a tremendous earthly Father!

To my husband, Benjamin "Sweetie" Page Browne, the priest of our home and the gatekeeper of my heart. You are truly the supporting cast of all that God asks me to do. Your belief in what God has called me to do is proven by your steadfast encouragement. Your prayers have gotten me through this process. Thank you for loving God first and me second. You have my heart. I love you!

Contents

Acclaim

FOR 31 DAYS OF SONSHINE

"This book is a gift. It is uplifting and insightful. This book is further evidence that God has gifted Dr. Janice with a tremendous love for others. Even in the midst of overwhelming grief she has shared her love for God and is using this as a ministry to heal the mind, soul, body, and spirit of those who will read this marvelous and beautifully written inspirational book."
Paula Blackwell, educator and author of *Lessons from My Hard Head: 52 Week Devotional*

"This book is a must read… The content is outstanding!"
Danny E. Blanchard, Ph.D., psychologist and author of *Well Water: Not My Real Name*

"Daily reading and meditating on Dr. Browne's uplifting messages will stimulate the reader's desire to embrace the light of Jesus which nurtures the mind, soul, body and spirit. For the mature Christian, the habit of basking in the Light, that may have become dimmed through personal loss, disappointment, pain, illness or time spent away from scriptural instruction, will be rekindled."
Elle Wharton, missionary, author, radio talk show host

"When Dr. Browne writes, we all need to pay attention. Her experience in the classroom, among peers, and in workplaces of the world agree. Take it from me, you will benefit from reading this marvelous book. Browne is always 'spot on'."
Charles E. Bradford, retired President North American Division of SDA and author of *Sabbath Roots, the African Connection*

"31 Days of SONshine is packed with encouraging, uplifting stories and laced with God's Word. It will challenge you to live life fully with joy no matter what. Dr. Browne shows that each big and little story of our lives matters. Not just for us personally but for each other and ultimately for Jesus. Soul inspiring!"
Emra Smith, speaker, trainer, life coach, and author of *Your Story Matters*

Foreword

I have known Dr. Janice "Jan" Johnson Browne my entire life. She is my cousin-sister, friend, and mentor. She has touched my life, spirit and soul for as long as I can remember. During my darkest days and most troubling times I always remembered Jan. Even when she was not in my physical presence she helped to shape my moral compass, spiritual direction and the essence of who I am today. My heart is full, and my spirit is even stronger from having her in my life.

I am inspired by Jan's book *31 Days of SONshine*. After reading her book it becomes very clear God has always proven faith will allow you to endure the tough times. Her daily readings are thought-provoking and filled with the Holy Spirit. When life is kicking you in the stomach and the devil is trying to stifle your spiritual growth, her daily thoughts and questions in each chapter will give you the strength to carry on. We have examples throughout the Bible and history that faith and an unrelenting belief in God will always help us to prevail.

Be it the call of Abraham or the commissioning of Moses, the leadership of Deborah, the witnessing of Esther, the anointing of David, they all triumphed through faith. Jan's inspiring words provide us with present-day life stories to remind us that we too can triumph through faith. *31 Days of SONshine* reminds us when your life is threatened, freedom is in jeopardy, hope is invisible, and evil seems triumphant, it is faith that will bring us through the tough times. The great prophets of the Bible and inspirational leaders throughout the generations knew that with God all things are possible.

Dr. Janice Browne's inspiring stories, anecdotes and testimonies confirm that though Moses is no match against a defiant pharaoh, David is insignificant to the giant Goliath, blind Sampson appears defeated by the Philistines and Paul is persecuted by his enemies, God still triumphs.

I am inspired by Dr. Jan's philosophical quotes at the end of each chapter and her thought provoking questions for the day. After participating in the *31 Days of SONshine* you will experience what I have had my entire life: the spiritual leadership, mentorship and guidance of Dr. Janice Johnson Browne.

Your life will be changed, your spirit will be rejuvenated, and your faith will be strengthened. There is a song that says:

I realize that sometimes in this life you're gonna be tossed by the waves and the
currents that seem so fierce,
but in the word of God I've got an anchor;
and it keeps me steadfast and unmovable despite the tide.
But if the storms don't cease,
and if the wind keeps on blowing,
my soul has been anchored in the Lord. ~Douglas Lee Miller

Copyright by RecordFly, LLC

After reading this book your soul will be anchored in the Lord. Do you need to change your life? Do you have a spiritual deficit? Do you want to be steadfast and unmovable despite the tide? Read this book and you will have the faith of a mustard seed to see you through the tough times and the difficulties of life.

Robert E. Johnson, Ph.D.
Chancellor, University of Massachusetts - Darmouth

Introduction

This book has been on my computer for a few years. I always intended to finish it, and have it published but never seemed to get around to it. Then something unfortunate happened which caused me to finally finish and publish this book, the untimely and unexpected deaths of my younger sister Cynthia and my youngest brother Grayland within a few weeks of each other. My dear sister fell asleep a few days before her next birthday and my brother was lowered into the ground on his birthday a sight almost too much to bear.

In the midst of tears and heartbreak I have finished this book and am doing what they both requested. I must share with you that rereading the manuscript has brought encouragement and healing for me. I never knew the stories I wrote to help others heal would become a healing balm for me. Only God could have let me live, write, and be encouraged by each story.

With anguish of heart and tears of deep sadness I look forward to a day of joy and peace. A day when God shall wipe away all tears from our eyes. John the Revelator writes in Revelation 21:4, *"And God shall wipe away all tears from their eyes; and there shall be no more death, neither sorrow, nor crying, neither shall there be any more pain: for the former things are passed away."* What a day! No more death, separation and grief. The stories and meditations in this book are healing for me, and I believe they will be for you.

"Weeping may endure for a night, but joy cometh in the morning"
Psalm 30:5

"But they that wait upon the Lord shall renew their strength; they shall mount up with wings as eagles; they shall run, and not be weary; and they shall walk, and not faint."
Isaiah 40:31

One beautiful spring day as I sat on our backyard deck basking in the warmth of the sun a loving feeling flowed over my entire being. As I closed my eyes and enjoyed those feelings, I thought in my mind this is how it feels when I experience blessings and miracles.

Each time I experience a blessing or a miracle I feel the warmth and love of the Son of God shinning on me. Wow! How wonderful it would be to have 31 uninterrupted beautiful days of sun shine. For this reason, I felt impressed to choose the book title 31 Days of SONshine.

For some of you, this will be a book of inspirational stories and meditations. For others it will be a devotional or daily spiritual guide. However, you choose to use it, be assured it will benefit you in positive ways. These stories, meditations, devotionals and daily spiritual guides will remind you that it's never too late to live your dream, that bullies are not always what they seem, doing something good for the rest of your life is inspiring to others, and sometimes you just need a good down-in-the-belly gut wrenching laugh. You will read about men and women who overcame adversity and earth-bound people who are angelic in their actions towards others.

Some stories will bring a smile to your face while others will soothe your hurt, move you to compassion, or inspire you to higher heights. The meditations will give you food for thought and treasures to carry in your heart. Some names have been changed but all 31 stories are true. May the SON always shine upon you as you meditate and receive a daily dose of SONshine.

My Commitment

With the help of God, I commit 31 days of my life for the healing of my mind, soul, body, and spirit.

Your Name

Janice Johnson Browne

I can do all things through Christ
which strengtheneth me.
Philippians 4:13

DAY 1

The Little Pear Tree

I will settle you after your old estates, and will do better unto you than at your beginnings: and ye shall know that I am the Lord.
- Ezekiel 36:11

That they might be called trees of righteousness, the planting of the Lord, that he might be glorified.
- Isaiah 61:3

Strong winds may blow into your life, they may shake your confidence and make you tremble, but with God's strength you will stand and be productive.
- Janice J. Browne

The papers were signed, the keys were in hand and soon we would be in our beautiful new, or shall I say, old home. It was more than 200 years old. We were so excited we could hardly wait to move in. Finally, the day came and here we were walking around on our beautiful acres of land. As we casually strolled around the grounds, my eyes were drawn to a small, spiny, thinly branched tree. Upon closer observation we experienced a wonderful surprise it was a pear tree!

Since it was October, we decided not to prune or trim anything until we could see what the grounds would look like in the spring. As the winter passed, spring came, and along with it spring showers and storms. One day as I looked out of our massive windows I could see dark, foreboding clouds, hail falling and trees bending. Suddenly I heard a loud clap of thunder and saw lightning bolts streaking through the sky. The next morning, I discovered my little pear tree had been struck by lightning.

"Oh no," I cried. "My tree! My little pear tree!" It has been struck by lightning.

The lightning struck the tree straight down the middle. The top fell off making it look like a bent, twisted, spiny branch sticking up from the ground. For days I mourned over my little tree.

In an effort to console me, my husband said, *"I am sorry about your tree. I guess we will just have to cut it down and I will plant another one for you."* With great sadness, I said *"No, for some reason I just do not want to cut it down."*

Time passed from that spring to the next spring. I became accustomed to looking at the tree each morning in its twisted state. Remarkably, as spring approached the branches looked a little stronger. One day, as I was looking out of the window, I noticed something different about my little pear tree. Guess what I saw? There were buds on the little pear tree. Upon closer inspection I saw the beginnings of leaves. Each day I watched the tree with eager anticipation. It looked rather funny, still twisted and bent over with a gap down the center, but with green leaves all over it.

A few days later, to my amazement, there were white flowers and eventually there were pears on the little tree! My tiny, frail, struck-by lightning tree was now bearing fruit! I could not believe my eyes!

The little pear tree was more beautiful than it was before it was struck by lightning. Yes, it was still twisted and bent, but beautiful in the sense that the white flowers seemed really bright; the leaves seemed greener; and to my utter surprise the fruit was larger than before! Within weeks the little pear tree was not only laden with fruit, it was now bending over from the weight. As the season progressed, our friends were able to come and get baskets of pears from that little tree.

I call this little tree my lesson tree because it taught me a lesson that I use in my daily life. Even though that tree was fragile as a result of being struck by lightning it did not give up and die. The tree weathered the storm, became stronger with each passing day and eventually overcame its weakness to bear large, sweet, delicious fruit again. What was the secret to this tree's success? In the midst of adversity, the tree remained connected to its roots.

We, too, must stay connected to our root, which is Jesus. He says in John 15:5, *"I am the vine, ye are the branches: He that abideth in me, and I in him, the same bringeth forth much fruit: for without me ye can do nothing."*

When you are tossed and turned, shattered by the cruelties of life until all hope seems gone, be assured that God is with you. He will give you perfect peace. He will guard your heart and mind, even in the midst of the storm. In Philippians 4:7, reassurance is offered. *"And the peace of God, which passeth all understanding, shall keep your hearts and minds through Christ Jesus."*

We, like that tree, are sometimes caught in the storms of life and struck by the lightning of sickness, grief, pain, trouble, heartbreak and countless burdens. We experience lightning bolts of trials and tribulations that crush our spirits.

We are bent, twisted, and it looks like we will never be the same or be productive again. But just like the tree we can't give up and die. God will provide the strength we need. In times of need read Isaiah 40:29, *"He giveth power to the faint; and to them that have no might he increaseth strength."* What a wonderful promise!

There is good news for us when we are struck by catastrophes. Despite the hardships, we can still bloom and bear fruit like that little pear tree. In due time, not only will you survive, you will thrive and be stronger than before. Just hold on and do not give up.

A Prayer for Today

Father God, help me to hold on through the storm. Your strength and love can help me to bloom when I feel I have nothing left. Thank you for your blessed assurance that you will help me through every storm. In the name of Jesus. Amen.

Questions for Reflection, Prayer, and Meditation

1. In this story we saw a storm almost destroy a tree. Sometimes we are almost destroyed by the storms of life. What storm(s) have you encountered that almost destroyed you? How did God help you to survive and even thrive?

_____

_____

_____

_____

_____

_____

_____

2. What did you learn from this story about restoration and renewal?

_____

_____

_____

_____

_____

_____

_____

3. What texts in this story provide the most encouragement for you when you go through the storms of life? Look up other texts that also may help in times of storms.

_____

_____

_____

_____

_____

_____

_____

YOUR RAY OF SONSHINE FOR TODAY:

*God is with you in your storm.
Not only will you survive, you will thrive.*

DAY 2
Doing Good

The rest of your life continues in heaven.

Janice J. Browne

Life is to be shared with others, spend the rest of it doing good.

Janice J. Browne

She wasn't very tall in stature, but she had one of the biggest hearts a human being could have. Her portfolio consisted of a tidy little house with adequate furnishings and outside plumbing. She wasn't a chef, but a bit of food always graced the table for anyone visiting. Each time I visited I was the recipient of nuts before I would end our visit.

My friend, Helen, who knew of my interest in helping orphaned children, introduced us and from the moment we met until the time I left Ethiopia we were fast friends. When I visited her, we would talk for hours. She would share with me her dreams, goals, and vision for the future. She would tell me time and time again, "I just want to live the rest of my life doing good."

She was a widow with no children of her own, but her house was filled with children of all ages. The small house had so many children in it she had to house some of them outside.

Their bedrooms outside of the house were large oil drums. Can you imagine sleeping in a large, cold, oily smelling oil drum? At night the oil drum was freezing cold and, in the day, it was sweltering hot. These were the best accommodations she had to offer them.

These children were orphaned in many ways. She picked some of them up from the side of the road; police would call her to come and get those that were abandoned at the police station; and others were dropped off by dying parents with HIV/AIDS.

There was no end to the calls she received yet no funds were given to her by anyone. She used the small pension left by her husband to feed and care for all of these orphaned children.

Many times, when my husband travelled to some other area of the country, he would stock up on the special food in that region and take it to the orphanage. She was most appreciative for the food and always, with tears in her eyes, thanked him. It was my humble privilege to take whatever I could to the children.

She followed the command given many years ago to the Israelites in Deuteronomy 15:11, *"For the poor shall never cease out of the land: therefore, I command thee, saying, Thou shalt open thine hand wide unto thy brother, to thy poor, and to thy needy, in thy land."*

In her heart she believed Psalm 127:3, *"Lo, children are an heritage of the Lord: and the fruit of the womb is his reward."* She did not birth them, but she loved them as if they were from her womb. In her heart she felt those children were her reward from God.

One evening as we sat and talked she told me how she started rescuing the children from their desperate situations. She remembered the circumstance of each child. When I asked why she felt the need to save these children she again repeated what she often said to me, "I just want to spend the rest of my life doing good."

I received the sad news that my friend died. It saddened my heart greatly, but I believe she lived out the rest of her life "doing good." As I reflect on her heart's desire of wanting to spend the rest of her life "doing good," I, too, want to do the same and pray each day for such an opportunity.

You, too, can spend the rest of your life "doing good" each day. You may not have an orphanage for children, but you can do good for children where you live. Children in need of love, care, mentoring, and education where you live. Let's make a pledge to spend the rest of our life "doing good."

A Prayer for Today

Father, you did so much good when you were on this earth. I want to touch others as you did. Please help me to spend the rest of my life doing good for others. In the name of Jesus. Amen.

Questions for Reflection, Prayer, and Meditation

1. Would you like to spend the rest of your life "doing good"? God will show you how. Write your personal request to God for the opportunity to do good wherever you are and whatever your circumstances.

_____

_____

_____

_____

_____

_____

_____

_____

2. What community organizations or programs are you aware of that are "doing good" by helping children and others? You may be able to help by donating funds, volunteering, or by praying for the organization. Write down specific ways you can "do good."

    _____

    _____

    _____

    _____

    _____

    _____

    _____

    _____

3. Write a prayer for the enduring strength of individuals and organizations who assist the needy and children as they continue "doing good."

    _____

    _____

    _____

    _____

    _____

    _____

    _____

    _____

YOUR RAY OF SONSHINE FOR TODAY

Make a conscious effort to "do good" the rest of your life.

DAY 3
Flowers in the Church

Faith is a flower that blooms in due season.
Janice J. Browne

Faith is a flower that blooms when the SON shines on it.
Janice J. Browne

It was a very sad time when the doors closed at Mary Rose's church. As the people left and the doors closed, my friend, Mary Rose, wept with bitter anguish and grief. Because of church enemies in her country's government, the church could no longer be open.

She always kept the green plants watered and the pews dusted when the church was open. What would she do now? How would her plants survive the heat and the cold? She thought carefully and devised a plan that would be a test and move of faith.

Even though it looked as if the doors would never open again, Mary Rose decided to pray and fast. She called a few of her friends together, and each day at noon they would pray for the church to re-open.

It did not seem sufficient to just pray and be idle. Mary Rose decided to climb through the back window of the church and take care of the flowers and church maintenance until the day the church would open again. She believed in her heart that one day she and her church members would be able to worship in freedom and peace again.

Her faith was severely tested when after nine... ten... eleven... months, the church remained closed. But Mary Rose determined in her heart to continue daily with her friends in prayer and fasting.

After one year of faith, the doors of the church did open again and that is where I worshiped each week with my husband who was the President of the Ethiopia Union Mission in Addis Ababa. After hearing the story, I felt so humbled to be sitting in a place that faith had opened. What seemed impossible to the human eye was more than possible through the eyes of God.

Mary Rose did not see evidence of the church opening, but she had hope. We read in Hebrews 11:1, *"Now faith is the substance of things hoped for, the evidence of things not seen."* Whatever you face in life whether it is a tragedy or a seemingly impossible situation, Luke 1:37, reassures us that, *"For with God nothing shall be impossible."*

A Prayer for Today

Dear Father, thank you for making the impossible possible through faith in you. Your power is magnificent, your grace is boundless, and your love for me is everlasting. Thank you for being a God of possibilities. In the name of Jesus. Amen.

Questions for Reflection, Prayer, and Meditation

1. When Mary Rose's faith was tested how did she react? When your faith is tested how do you react? How can you allow God to help you as you go through your test of faith?

_____

_____

_____

_____
_____
_____
_____
_____

2. Reflect and meditate on the text(s) in the story that you feel can most encourage you in your time of testing.

_____
_____
_____
_____
_____
_____
_____
_____
_____

3. Write a short prayer thanking God for helping you through the times your faith was tested and ask Him to help you in your present time of testing.

_____
_____
_____
_____
_____
_____
_____
_____
_____

YOUR RAY OF SONSHINE FOR TODAY

Hold on!
You may shed many tears
but don't give up!
God will reward you
for your faith!

DAY 4
A House of Pain

He healeth the broken in heart, and bindeth up their wounds.
Psalm 147:3

God takes the pain, wraps it in His heart, and suffers with us.
Janice J. Browne

My sisters and I absolutely love beauty in all forms. We love the beauty of God, people, nature, architecture, and interior design. We enjoy looking at beautifully decorated houses with well-manicured lawns and breathtaking flower gardens.

As we tour these houses, family pictures are displayed that reflect love, joy and peace. Some pictures are memories of family vacations. Others are portraits of the entire family, showing the progression of the generations. These pictures always bring joy to my heart as I imagine an affectionate family that was happy like the six of us as we grew up with our loving mother and father.

One Sunday afternoon my sister, Stephanie, my nephew Andrew, and I visited the kind of home I have described. This house was magnificent! Room after room was lavishly furnished with all of the amenities imaginable. There was a kitchen closet the size of a banquet hall, full of silver. The staff was working diligently, smiled and nodded politely as the realtor guided us on the tour.

The realtor showed us the features of the house and proceeded to share some of the history of the family and the house. We learned that the owners were now deceased; the most recent being the wife who had transitioned just three weeks prior to this house showing. The husband and wife were both from wealthy families and had everything their hearts could desire. This house was truly a mansion.

As we toured the house I reflected on the promise that one day I, too, will live in a mansion built by my heavenly Father. John 14: 2- 3 reads, *"In my Father's house are many mansions: if it were not so, I would have told you. I go to prepare a place for you. And if I go and prepare a place for you, I will come again, and receive you unto myself; that where I am, there ye may be also."* A mansion in my Father's house!

As we continued to walk through the house we asked questions about the structure, the foundation and other important details. The foundation was sound, the structure was firm, and the house was well maintained.

After being satisfied with the answers to our foundational questions, we inquired about the pictures of the owner's two beautiful daughters who looked to be in their early twenties. As we admired their beauty, the realtor, with a very sad look, told us the daughter with the dark hair had completed suicide after many attempts and a lengthy addiction to drugs. The one with the fair hair was the seller of the house along with all its contents included and never wanted to step foot in it again.

She had not visited in years and wouldn't even return to sell the house. It was sad to imagine what pain there must have been in that house even though, from all appearances, everything looked perfect.

Our tour brought us to an enormous closet divided into five sections. Each section housed the mistress's wardrobe. Every designer label one could want was in that closet. There were endless rows of hats, dresses, formal gowns, as well as coats, belts, purses, and accessories to match every outfit.

Then something struck us as being surprisingly different. Within the rows of beautiful and expensive shoes there was only one shoe of each kind. We didn't see a matching shoe. My astute little nephew made the observation and asked about the mate to each of the shoes.

The realtor explained, "Sadly, the owner had only one leg. When she was in her twenties she developed cancer in her knee and eventually her leg had to be removed. She lived out her days with only one leg."

As we left the house we thanked the realtor for the tour and my sister told her she would be in touch. When we got into the car we had prayer for the remaining daughter, asking God to be with her and to heal any broken places in her heart. Stephanie said she loved the house and asked Andrew what he thought about it and if he'd like to live there.

"No Mom," he decisively replied. "That house is a house full of pain."

What appeared to be a wonderfully cheerful exquisite home was, in reality, a sad, depressing and joyless house. One never knows the hardships others are enduring. They may appear to be happy or seem to have everything and be in control of their life, but that may not be the case.

One day the trial, pain and suffering will all end. It won't always be this way. "And God shall wipe away all tears from their eyes; and there shall be no more death, neither sorrow, nor crying, neither shall there be any more pain: for the former things are passed away" (Revelation 21:4). We will live in a pain-free atmosphere designed by our Father just for us!

We will walk on streets of gold. "And the street of the city was pure gold" (Revelation 21:21). We will wear custom designed crowns of life created by Jesus, James 1:12. What a designer crown - a crown with life in it!

A Prayer for Today

Father, I pray for myself and others who are in deep spiritual, emotional, financial, or physical pain. I pray for the daughter in this story, and for others who are in terrible situations. Help me to give you the pain. Please help me hold on to you and when you shall come, please help me to be ready to meet you in peace. My desire is to live in our beautiful mansions pain free forever with you. In the name of Jesus. Amen.

Questions for Reflection, Prayer, and Meditation

1. Reflect on this story. What stood out to you in this story?

_____

_____

_____

_____

_____

_____

_____

_____

2. Which of the scriptures in the story have been most comforting to you as you have gone through the pain sometimes experienced in life?

_____

_____

_____

_____

_____

_____

_____

_____

3. Pray for someone today who seems to have it all and write a prayer of gratitude for what God has done for you.

_____

_____

_____

_____

YOUR RAY OF SONSHINE FOR TODAY

*Your pain
will not last forever.*

DAY 5

Job, Bees, and Ants

*A day without appreciating the beauty of
God's creation is a day without SONshine.*
Janice J. Browne

*Go to the ant, thou sluggard; consider her ways, and be wise: Which having no guide,
overseer, or ruler, Provideth her meat in the summer, and gathereth her food in the harvest.*
Proverbs 6:6–8

The ants are a people not strong, yet they prepare their meat in the summer.
Proverbs 30:25

When the Holy Spirit impressed me with the title of this devotional I had to laugh out loud. I am sure when you read the title of this devotional you probably thought to yourself "I don't remember reading about any bees or ants in the story of Job.

Well, this story is not about the Job that we read about in the Bible. It is the story of a young man named Eyob the Amharic name which when translated to English is Job. Job was a wonderful hardworking young man in Ethiopia whom God sent to us as a friend, son, and lover of God's earth and all His creation. We had the most beautiful yard on the compound thanks to Job.

Job took special care of the roses, bushes, grass, and insects. Yes, the insects! Job was very knowledgeable and respectful of all of God's creatures including the ants. His love of God's nature was astounding and the knowledge he had acquired about nature was even more astounding.

One day we were all sitting in the house talking when someone rang the doorbell. When I opened the door for our visitor, a bee flew into the house.

The bee didn't sound very happy as he found himself trapped inside the house. It began to buzz around the room in circles. I shrieked in fear of suffering a bee sting and everyone else ran for cover except Job. He stood calmly in the middle of the room without saying a word then stretched out his hand and waited quietly for the bee to come to him.

As the rest of us peeked around the corner, the bee flew around the room once more, then calmly landed in the middle of Job's hand. Job gently cupped his hand and began to talk to the bee for a minute or so. He then walked calmly to the door and said good-bye to the bee. I was amazed at what I saw and in awe at the beauty of Job's tenderness, kindness, and interaction with God's creation.

On another occasion I witnessed Job's friendship with God's creatures. It was summertime in Ethiopia and this particular year was the year of the fire ants. And when I say fire ants I mean ants with fire in their sting. Just the thought of them makes me itch all over!

We had many encounters as I trampled over them to hang my freshly washed clothes on the outdoor clothes line. I became so disgusted with the long trail of ants in my backyard that I decided I would ask Job to buy some ant killer when he came to the house.

As soon as Job arrived I made my request to him. But he did not respond in his customary helpful way. Instead he looked surprised and wanted to know why I needed the ant killer. "Well," I said, "because the ants are making a long trail across my backyard." Job calmly responded, "Yes because they are on a journey to prepare for the winter."

Okay, so they are on a journey.

Job went on to say, "They are not at war with you. If you'll notice, they are in a straight line following the leader just passing through. You keep stepping on them and breaking up their line which really isn't in your way."

Okay, they are not in my way.

I thought about what Job said and he was right. They were not in my way. They were just passing through and all I had to do was step over the very small thin line on my way to the clothes line. It all began to make sense. Job also told me that since they were only passing through it would be over in about seven more days.

Well, guess who started counting?

Guess how many days passed? You guessed it! In exactly seven days the line of ants no longer existed. They were gone!

When I think about Job and God's creatures I think about how God tenderly holds us in His hands and leads us out of trouble. One of my favorite chapters in the Bible is Psalm 23 that reminds us that even when we walk through the valley of the shadow of death we need not fear any evil.

I also think about how sometimes on a life journey our journey is interrupted. Isaiah 43:2 reads, *"When thou passesth through the waters, I will be with thee; and through the rivers, they shall not overflow thee: when thou walkest through the fire, thou shalt not be burned; neither shall the flame kindle upon thee."* No need to fear He will keep His arms around you on the journey. Someone may step on you and crush you down, but God will pick you up and put you back on the right path. Just trust and obey Him. Stay focused. Don't give up.

But mostly I think about the fact that one day in the earth made new, we are not going to be at war and in fear of God's creatures. Isaiah 11:6-7 reads, *"The wolf also shall dwell with the lamb, and the leopard shall lie down with the kid; and the calf and the young lion and the fatling together; and a little child shall lead them. And the cow and the bear shall feed; their young ones shall lie down together: and the lion shall eat straw like the ox."*

The bees will no longer sting, and the ants will no longer bite!

What a glorious day that will be!
The song "Peace in The Valley" says it beautifully:

Well the bear will be gentle, and the wolf will be tame, and the lion shall lay down, down by the lamb, oh yes and the beasts from the wild Shall be led by a child And I'll be changed, changed from this creature that I am, oh yes.

~Thomas A. Dorsey

A Prayer for Today

Father, I thank you for all of your beautiful creatures and creation on this earth. Help me to be ready when you return so that I can lie down peacefully with all of your creation, ants included. In the name of Jesus. Amen!

Questions for Reflection, Prayer, and Meditation

1. What did you glean from this story?

   _____

   _____

   _____

   _____

   _____

   _____

   _____

   _____

2. Do you view God's creation differently after reading this story?

   _____

   _____

   _____

   _____

   _____

   _____

   _____

3. Reflect on how God holds you tenderly in the palm of His hands and write a prayer of thanks.

_____

_____

_____

_____

_____

_____

_____

YOUR RAY OF SONSHINE FOR TODAY

*Open your heart
to God's gift of
creation designed
just for you.*

DAY 6
Angels on Earth

Angels are not afraid to go with us wherever we are sent.
Janice J. Browne

Angels are with us and in the most interesting places in the world.
Janice J. Browne

While serving in the mission field, my husband and I were considering adopting a young Ethiopian girl. We were told by Harigowane the orphanage owner that we should talk to the person who had rescued her from a large group of people outside of their compound gate.

Harigowane told us that each morning hundreds of desperate people would stand crying and begging for food and shelter at the Brothers of Charity gate. This young girl was one of the people in that crowd. When the gates were opened she was admitted into the compound but because the facility only housed males, she was immediately brought to Harigowane's orphanage.

I called the Brothers of Charity Compound and was given an appointment for the following week. We looked forward with eager anticipation to the scheduled appointment. As we drove through the compound gates, we were startled by what we saw. They were human forms but distorted with such deformities that they looked frightening to the eyes. Some had no eyes. Others had one eye, but it was located in their forehead. Their limbs were twisted and bent in directions that didn't seem possible. Their faces were totally disfigured. As we drove in and parked they all came to the car and began to look in the window, placing their deformed hands and pressing their contorted faces on the window. Saliva dripped down some of their mouths. Some could hardly walk so they dragged themselves to the car.

As I looked at them with sadness deeper than almost anything I could remember, I noticed that even though their faces were deformed and crooked, they were smiling— a crooked smile but a smile none-the-less. They were welcoming us!

I quickly got out of the car and began to hug them when a very neatly dressed, extraordinarily handsome man with beautiful eyes, hair, skin, and a lovely smile walked towards us. He looked like how I imagined an angel would look; perfectly formed in every way. His movements were calm and heavenly-like, gentleness and kindness flowed through him. He introduced himself as one of the Brothers of Charity and warmly welcomed my husband and me to the compound.

As we sat and chatted with Brother John about the possibility of adopting the girl, the conversation changed. We learned that he and two other men represented the Brothers of Charity, an organization that takes care of the less fortunate around the world. He was from India and the other Brothers were from Kenya and Ethiopia. They were the lone caretakers for these poor, unfortunate souls. I was further touched when, in answer to my question as to how long he would be at the compound, with kindness he answered, "For the rest of my life."

He made a vow to care for the residents until his own death. The two other Brothers of Charity had made that same vow. They would care for the people at the compound until their own death.

As we toured the compound I noticed that he treated the residents with the utmost kindness and compassion. He would wipe the saliva from their mouth with a handkerchief from his pocket or pat them on their shoulders.

He took us to a room where the more severely incapacitated lived. These people were unable to care for their bodily needs. They were totally dependent upon their caretakers.

The Brothers of Charity would take turns bathing the residents and cleaning their living area twenty-four hours each day, seven days a week. The room, which should otherwise have been smelly and dirty, was spotless.

My eyes fill with tears each time I think of that visit, the people, and the angelic kindness of the Brothers of Charity. If ever there were angels on earth they would be the Brothers of Charity. I feel so honored to have met these angels and God's children whom they love and take care of each day. God tells us in His word that we are to care for those less fortunate than ourselves.

One day Jesus the King of Kings will say, *"Come, ye blessed of my Father, inherit the kingdom prepared for you from the foundation of the world: For I was an hungry, and ye gave me meat: I was thirsty, and ye gave me drink: I was a stranger, and ye took me in: Naked, and ye clothed me: I was sick, and ye visited me: I was in prison, and ye came unto me"* (Matthew 25:34-36).

This visit also reminds me of how crooked and deformed we are by sin and how Jesus came to this world, touching the deformed with gentleness, love, and compassion. How long did he stay? He stayed until He died. But He rose from the dead (Mark 16:6). He is coming back to this earth and every eye shall see Him (Revelation 1:7).

Will you pray each day with me for the Brothers of Charity and others like them who have given their lives to care for some of the most unfortunate people in the world? God bless the Brothers of Charity and God bless you for praying for them.

A Prayer for Today

Dearest Father, loving Jesus, and precious Holy Spirit, please bless the Brothers of Charity in Ethiopia and around the world. Bless those who are in their care until you come and take away all sickness, sadness, and sorrow. In the name of Jesus. Amen, amen, and amen!

Questions for Reflection, Prayer, and Meditation

1. Take a moment and reflect on the compassion shown by the Brothers of Charity then write how God shows you compassion.

   _____

   _____

   _____

   _____

   _____

   _____

   _____

   _____

2. You may or may not feel you have been called for such a mission as the "angels" mentioned in today's meditation. But what can you do on a local level to help relieve or reduce the suffering of those who are less fortunate?

   _____

   _____

   _____

   _____

   _____

   _____

   _____

   _____

3. According to the request in today's devotional, will you say a prayer at this moment and pray on a regular basis for the worldwide work of the Brothers of Charity?

   _____

   _____

   _____

   _____

   _____

YOUR RAY OF SONSHINE FOR TODAY

*Perform courageous
acts of charity.*

DAY 7

The Bully

Bullies are scared little people who, deep inside, feel bad about themselves.
Janice J. Browne

Never let a bully see you sweat; it will make them sweat.
Janice J. Browne

She could not have been much taller than us nor was she much older; in fact, she was only one year older and actually the same size. But you would have to know her in order to understand why she seemed to be six feet tall and much older. She was the bully.

This is where the story begins. We could hardly wait for the bell to ring indicating that it was the noon recess time. It was a lovely spring day, and the happy laughter of children, balls bouncing, and the fun of jumping rope bought joy to our young hearts.

Then it happened, as I was turning the rope on one end and my friend the other, without warning, the bully walked straight through the middle of the turning rope. The look of satisfaction at stopping our fun was almost unbearable. As she triumphantly walked away, I took the rope and flung the end of it at her in the pretense of hitting her, not thinking that she would turn around, but at that moment, she turned around, and the rope hit her in the face leaving a big red mark.

Oh, no! I didn't mean to hit her. I was just making a motion of pretense at hitting her. I was petrified and frozen with fear. I could see the angry glare in her eyes. Then something else happened, the bell rang signaling us that recess was over, and it was time to go inside. Whew! The bell rang just in time. Everyone started to chant, "Saved by the bell, just by the bell." I knew what that meant.

If that bell had not rung, I was going to be chopped meat.

As we went inside, I could feel the tension. Our classmates made note of the incident and every chance they got, they made sure we knew that this was not over and would be finished when the bell rang to end school for the day. Each time the teacher left the classroom, the class would say, "Oh boy, there's going to be a fight!" This went on for the rest of the day.

We had two hours to go before school would end. One hour went by, and then it was just a few more minutes before it would be time to go home. Everybody was ready to see the big showdown the big bully and poor little me. My throat was dry, my eyes were wide with fear and the hair on my head felt as if it were standing on end.

Then the bell rang, and without explanation or reason the bully jumped out of her seat and ran out of the door, leaving us all wondering what happened. Well I had to go outside, and everyone made sure I did by saying, "She's waiting for you." I prayed and prayed then resigned myself to the task ahead.

As I stepped outside, I couldn't see her, nor could anyone else. She was wildly running down the street. She was afraid and ran away with all the speed she could muster. The bully was not as tough as we thought. I couldn't believe it!! God had heard my prayer. I would not be chopped meat that day or any other.

Everyone was shocked, especially me. God had fought my battle. God continues to fight my battles each day. When she did return to school a few days later, I made an apology and we became lifelong friends. She was no longer a bully, and I was hailed as a hero, but it was not me who was the hero, it was God who fought the battle for me.

This journey back to my childhood reminds me of the bullies we face as adults. We face bullies of pressure, tension, anxiety, intimidation, fear, gossip, angry people, sickness, financial burdens, and the list goes on and on. These bullies are just waiting to beat us up, but they are not as tough as they seem. We do not have to be afraid of bullies. God will fight our battles for us.

It is comforting to know that the same promise and instruction that was given to the inhabitants of Judah and Jerusalem is true for us today. *"And he said, Harken ye, all Judah, and yes inhabitants of Jerusalem, and thou King Jehoshaphat, Thus saith the LORD unto you, Be not afraid nor dismayed by reason of this great multitude; for the battle is not yours, but God's"* (2 Chronicles 20:15).

When bullies come don't be afraid nor dismayed. Sometimes all we need to do is stand still as God instructed in 2 Chronicles 20:17, *"Ye shall not need to fight in this battle: set yourselves, stand ye still, and see the salvation of the Lord with you…fear not, nor be dismayed…for the Lord will be with you."*

God is with us in our battles.

For three and a half years, Jesus dealt with a bully on this earth, the same bully He had encountered in heaven before the bully was cast out to the earth. Another showdown took place at Calvary more than two thousand years ago; God fought the bully at the cross and won. Jesus fought and won. Jesus said in Revelation 1:8, 18, *"I am Alpha and Omega, the beginning and the ending, …I am He that liveth, and was dead; and, behold, I am alive for evermore, amen; and have the keys of hell and of death."*

You do not have to be afraid or worry about the bullies of this life. Stand still. Let God fight the bully because the battle is not yours, it is the Lords, and the victory has already been won through Jesus Christ our Lord. Hallelujah!

A Payer for Today

Dearest Jesus, sometimes we run away filled with fear only to find that you have already won the battle. Thank you for fighting and winning all of our battles for us. Amen.

Questions for Reflection, Prayer, and Meditation

1. Have you ever been bullied? You are no longer that bullied person. God helped you through the fearful situation. It's over. Ask God to help you to forgive the bully. Pray for your healing and for the healing of the bully. Write your prayer here.

_____
_____
_____
_____
_____
_____
_____
_____
_____

2. Are you a bully? Have you ever been a bully? Repent, and write a prayer asking God to forgive you for what you did to the person(s) you bullied.

_____
_____
_____
_____
_____
_____
_____
_____
_____

3. Think of all the children and other persons who are being bullied even at this moment. I am asking that you stop and pray for them now. I am also asking you to be a change agent. Stop bullying when you see it. Write your prayer below.

_____

_____

_____

_____

_____

_____

_____

_____

_____

YOUR RAY OF SONSHINE FOR TODAY

*You are free
of being bullied
and released
from being a bully.*

DAY 8

A Piece of Junk

There is beauty in you.
Janice J. Browne

There is treasure inside of you that has yet to be revealed.
Janice J. Browne

Let the creator bring out the beauty in you.
Janice J. Browne

It sat amid the manure and hay right next to the horse stall and everything that inhabits a barn. We did not have a garage attached to our 200 plus year-old house, so we used a portion of the barn as our garage just in front of the horse trough. Interesting to imagine, isn't it? Well, it gets more interesting as the story unfolds.

Each time we drove the car into the barn, to our left sat a dirty, ragged, frame of what used to be a lovely antique sofa. The wood was chipped, cracked, and bore scars from many days gone by. The springs popped out from every direction and it had a lean to the left that made it look hopelessly pitiful.

Each time I looked at the remains of the sofa, I said to myself, "That sofa has done its job. It is time for a permanent rest at the nearest garbage dump." My husband asked me, "Why are we keeping that sofa?" With a look of genuine sincerity, he said, "That sofa is just a piece of junk." I sweetly reminded him that it belonged to my mother who requested we keep it there until she made arrangements for it to be delivered to the city where she lived.

One day we received a call from my mother telling us that someone would be coming to pick up the sofa and deliver it to her. I can't say we were sad to see it go, and I wondered what she would do with it. After all, it was just a piece of junk.

Time went by, we would visit my parents and on one visit we noticed a new piece of furniture sitting in my parent's Master's Suite. It was a beautiful, elegant, stately white sofa. The white wooden legs, trimmed in gold, were beautifully polished, the silk fabric that covered it was exquisite, and it sat elegantly in the room.

The sofa was quite a beautiful sight to behold. It looked new. It reminded me of the Bible text in 2 Corinthians 5:17 that reads, *"Therefore if any man be in Christ, he is a new creature: old things are passed away; behold, all things are become new."*

God can recreate us, we become new!

Yes, it was the piece of junk we had housed in our barn. We could not believe our eyes! What we had seen as just a piece of junk was now valuable. My mother had a different view of the sofa than we had. She saw it in a state of beauty--a beautiful, strikingly elegant piece of useful furniture. She had vision where we had none.

She saw past the dirt, filth, and brokenness. Her vision was for that sofa to be beautiful and useful again. This story reminds me of how we sometimes see ourselves and how God sees us. There may be times when we see ourselves or others see us as just a piece of junk. But God sees us as beautiful and worth saving. God created us and knows everything about us. *"Oh Lord, thou hast searched me and known me, Thou knowest my downsitting and mine uprising, thou understandest my thought afar off. Thou hast beset me behind and before, and laid thine hand upon me"* (Psalm 139: 1, 2, 5).

God's vision of and for us is beautiful and useful. *"I will praise thee; for I am fearfully and wonderfully made: marvelous are thy works; and that my soul knoweth right well" (Psalm 139: 14).*

Just like the upholsterer put that piece of junk back together and made it a desirable beautiful piece of furniture. So, it is with God. We may be broken, leaning, unsightly and seeming good for nothing, but God the Master Upholsterer remakes and covers us with His beautiful righteousness.

We become desirable and useful in His service! Each time I visit my mother and we sit on the sofa together, I think about this story and how God used a sofa and my mother to teach me about the power of God's recreation of me and each of us.

I love sitting on that sofa and talking to my mother about the love of God. *"Behold, what manner of love the Father hath bestowed upon us, that we should be called the sons of God: therefore, the world knoweth us not, because it knew him not" (1 John 3:1).* What love! Even unto death! *"For God so loved the world, that he gave his only begotten Son, that whosoever believeth in him should not perish, but have everlasting life" (John 3:16).*

A Prayer for You Today

Father, I thank you for recreating me into your lovely image. I am dust created in your magnificent image. The love that you have for me is so amazing and abundant. I praise you for your grace and mercy. Amen.

Questions for Reflection, Prayer, and Meditation

1. While reading this story, how were you enlightened about your personal value?

   _____
   _____
   _____
   _____
   _____
   _____
   _____
   _____
   _____
   _____

2. Do you see others as valuable? How can you see value in others and how can you bring out the value in others?

   _____
   _____
   _____
   _____
   _____
   _____
   _____
   _____
   _____
   _____

3. Write down how God has recreated, changed, and reinvented you. You may instead, or also, write a prayer asking God to re-create, renew, change, and show you your value.

   _____
   _____
   _____
   _____
   _____
   _____

YOUR RAY OF SONSHINE FOR TODAY

God sees past our dirt, filth, and brokenness.

DAY 9

There is No Love in This Card

A friend loveth at all times.
Proverbs 17:17

It is good to see love in action, it helps us to feel it.
Janice J. Browne

You may write about it, sing about it, even say it, but love is an action word.
Janice J. Browne

My friend Marion's grandniece is an awesome little girl. Marion once told me a story about her grandniece that I thought was outstanding. It was Marion's grandnieces seventh birthday. Her mother was very excited and set out to make her birthday a grand celebration! Many of her relatives came to the birthday party and brought presents, cards, and lots of love! Everyone seemed to have a wonderful time at the party. Marion's grandniece was all smiles and laughter. After everyone was filled with ice cream and cake, it was time to open her many presents. This was the moment she had been waiting for and now it was here!

As she opened presents of every size and shape you could hear her tiny voice full of joy and laughter saying, "Thank you, I love it!" She also received many cards and opened each one and read it so that everyone could hear the message of the card. As she read each card her sweet and sincere little voice would end by reading the words "With Love" and the signature of the person who gave her the card.

She continued in this way reading card after card until something different happened. She opened the card, read the message, and a name signed at the bottom. To everyone's surprise she looked sad, then said in a very disappointed voice, "Mommy, there's no love in this card." Wow! Did you read those words she expressed?

There is no love in this card.

The words of that little girl remind me that sometimes we do things for people without love and cheerfulness. We also take that same attitude with God. We give to worthy charities, some of us give tithe and offerings to our church, or we may contribute to a child's school project, you know, buy the candy, but there is no love in it.

We are not cheerful givers. We give grudgingly. *"Give, and it shall be given unto you; good measure, pressed down, and shaken together, and running over, shall men give into your bosom. For with the same measure that ye mete withal it shall be measured to you again" (Luke 6:38).*

Wow! There is also a promised attached for cheerful givers.

The way you give will come back to you. If you give in abundance with love it will come back to you. God loves a cheerful giver. There should be "love" in the giving.

Just think the Father gave His only begotten Son to die for us, what love there was in His heart. Jesus gave His life with love in it! *"For God so loved the world, that He gave His only begotten son, that whosoever believeth in Him should not perish, but have everlasting life" (John 3:16).*

Jesus came to the earth, lived, and died for us so that we could be saved through His eternal blood. What love! He came that you might have life and have it more abundantly. He gave abundantly! He does not take from us instead He gives. *"The thief cometh not, but for to steal, and to kill, and to destroy: I am come that they might have life, and that they might have it more abundantly" (John 10: 10).* I don't want to do things for God or others with no love in it. God wants our whole heart, and He wants our love to be in it.

A Prayer for Today

Dear Father, help us do everything with love in it. Amen.

Questions for Reflection, Prayer, and Meditation

1. There is a difference between things done or given in love and acts that are not done or given in love. How do you feel when you experienced genuine love, when something is given or done for you? How do you feel when the person just does it for you out of obligation with no love in it?

_____

_____

_____

_____

_____

_____

_____

_____

_____

2. Rethink how and why you do things for others and how it affects them and you. If you have given something to someone or done something for someone without love, ask God to enlighten your mind on how to authentically do for others and give with genuine love.

_____
_____
_____
_____
_____
_____
_____
_____
_____

3. Now that you've read this story, I challenge you to do something for someone without complaint, anger, hostility, or bare necessity.

_____
_____
_____
_____
_____
_____
_____
_____
_____

YOUR RAY OF SONSHINE FOR TODAY

The Bible,
your greeting card from God,
is overflowing with love
and is waiting for you
to open it today. It is signed,
With love,
God

DAY 10
A New Heart

Keep they heart with all diligence; for out of it are the issues of life.
Proverbs 4:23

Even when the heart is old love doesn't get old it remains young forever.
Janice J. Browne

Love is great exercise for the heart muscle.
Janice J. Browne

Your heart becomes new each time it loves.
Janice J. Browne

I was visiting my brother, sister-in-law and nephew Trey in California. Each day I had the joy of going with my brother to pick my nephew up from school. He was always happy, full of energy, and had lots to share with us about his day and all of his activities. One day we picked him up from school and noticed he was not the usual, energetic, happy boy we'd seen each day. His father and I looked at each other as if to say, that is not our Trey as he slowly walked to the car.

Once he was in the car we began to ask him about his day at school to which he replied, "Oh, it was ok." We asked if anything was wrong because to us he seemed a little sad. That is when he told us that he was very sad because the teacher told them that their classmate had a heart condition and was very sick. She also shared with them that her heart condition was very serious and that she might not be able to run and play with them the way she use to at school. The teacher asked each of them to pray for their classmate.

We reassured him as best we could in every way. We told him that we would pray and that he needed to pray for his friend also. In fact, we decided to stop right then and there to have prayer for his classmate. He seemed to perk up a little but still seemed sad and down about the situation.

As we road home we were all very quiet. We were all praying in our hearts. When we got home, Trey went straight to his room without another word. As the evening passed it was time for dinner and family worship. We gathered at the table and ate dinner in silence. After dinner we all sat in the family room for worship. Trey's Dad had opening prayer and read from the Bible *"And it shall come to pass, that before they call, I will answer; and while they are yet speaking I will hear"* *(Isaiah 65:24).*

His father assured him that God knew about the situation and was working on healing his friend's heart. We each offered words of encouragement about God hearing our prayers for his friend. After we shared our thoughts and texts on God answering prayer, we all knelt to pray.

I will never forget the prayer that Trey prayed. With complete faith, trust, and childlike innocence Trey simply prayed "Dear Father give my friend a new heart." He didn't pray for her heart to get healed or for her to get well. He very earnestly and simply prayed for her to have a "new heart."

Those words and that request were so profound. I thought about those words over and over. Give her a new heart...a new heart. That is what we all need, a new heart. If we ask God for a new heart He will give it to us and fill it with peace, love, joy, and happiness.

A Prayer for Today

Dear Father, give me a new heart filled with all of your precious gifts from your heart to ours. Amen.

Questions for Reflection, Prayer, and Meditation

1. What is the life lesson in this story?

   _____

   _____

   _____

   _____

   _____

   _____

   _____

   _____

   _____

2. Meditate on what having a new heart means to you?

   _____

   _____

   _____

   _____

   _____

   _____

   _____

   _____

   _____

3. Write a prayer request for a new heart.

_____

_____

_____

_____

_____

_____

_____

_____

_____

YOUR RAY OF SONSHINE FOR TODAY

Exercise your heart
by using it to love.

DAY 11
A Journey of Love

If you let God's love fill your heart it will flow out to others.
Janice J. Browne

The journey of love begins at the start of each new day.
Janice J. Browne

*L*iving in Ethiopia was one of the most spiritual exciting, educational, diverse experiences of my life! I loved the people, culture, traditions, food, dress, and the holidays. My favorite holiday was Timkat. It is the Ethiopian Orthodox Christian's celebration of the baptism of Jesus by John the Baptist in the Jordan River.

This festival is a ritual reenactment of baptism similar to reenactments performed by numerous Christian pilgrims to the Holy Land when they visit the Jordan River and are baptized as a commemoration of their first baptism. During this three-day celebration the mood throughout Ethiopia and in Addis Ababa where we lived, is festive, joyful, and full of singing and laughter. It is the most colorful, festive holiday of them all. The clothes that are worn reflect bright colors and lots of details in the making of the garments. The poor as well as the rich put on their best and head to a large park where tent after tent is filled with an assortment of food and souvenirs, people singing, praying, and families sitting together soaking up the atmosphere.

At the end of each day everyone heads home, and the celebration continues. The food is plenteous, the laughter is hardier, and the children are frolicking everywhere with their friends as if this is the last day they will ever be together. And when you think about it, it will never be the same day, nor will they be the same age ever again. As I watched them so happy, carefree, and filled with energy I said a prayer for each of them.

We along with other Ethiopians on that day celebrated the memory of Jesus's baptism by John the Baptist as found in John 1:9-11.

It was a day of celebration and sharing with neighbors and friends. The housekeeper made sure that the house was sparkling, the lawn keeper made sure that the yard was manicured to perfection and we welcomed everyone who wanted to come and eat with us. This special day reminded me of Christmas in so many ways and caused me to reminisce about my home and family so far away in America.

But the story in the story is the young girl who we took into our home from an orphanage. She stayed with us until her schooling ended at which time we sent her to a boarding academy for further education. She was a lovely girl and very grateful for our kindness to her. She voluntarily and delightfully cooked our food for that special day and made a variety of dishes.

Our favorite was Ethiopian spicy red lentil pottage. The lentils were so good that an Ethiopian neighbor told me that legend has it that Esau sold his birthright to Jacob for those beans! Read the story in Genesis 25:29-34. The lentils were delicious but not delicious enough to sell our birthright for them!

As she prepared the variety of dishes she came to me very concerned and told me that one of the most special dishes for the day was not prepared and that because it had to be prepared in a special way she would need to go to a friend's house to prepare it. I told her that it wasn't necessary to go to that kind of trouble, but she insisted and quickly left the house.

She must have been gone for about two hours. When she returned, we noticed that she had a very large heavy dark metal pot on her shoulder filled with the specially prepared greens. This may not sound like much to you but let me share more with you about her journey to get the special dish for us.

She walked on foot approximately five miles each way, over very rough terrain alone with a large steel pot that weighed about four pounds empty and with the added greens even more!

When we saw her approach the house our hearts were touched by her love and dedication. There she was a petite young girl with a heavy burden on her shoulders that she carried all that way to show her love for us. This story brings tears to my eyes because she loved us so much she carried that burden for miles and miles just for us!

There is someone else who loves you very much and carried a very heavy burden all the way to the cross. He did it just for you and me. What Love!

He carries our grief, sorrows, pains, trials, troubles, and sicknesses. *"But he was wounded for our transgressions, he was bruised for our iniquities: the chastisement of our peace was upon him; and with his stripes we are healed" (Isaiah 53:5)*. His name is Jesus.

Jesus carried the old rugged, heavy, splintered cross over the miles just for us so that we can have eternal life with Him. Thank you, Jesus! He started his journey in humble beginnings wrapped in swaddling clothes and lying in a manger (Luke 2:7). His next stop on the journey was the Garden of Gethsemane where he was betrayed by a kiss an act that represents kindness and love from someone (Mark 14:43-44). The earthly journey ended as he walked the rugged, rough terrain, alone with the burden of a heavy cross upon His shoulders showing His unbelievable love for us! An innocent man was crucified. The Creator was crucified by the creation (Mark 15:25).

The young girl walked miles with the heavy burden because she wanted to show us her love. Jesus walked miles with the heavy burden of the cross and showed us His love. What a journey of love!

A Prayer for Today

Jesus, thank you for the unbelievable journey of love you traveled from heaven to earth just for me. Amen.

Questions for Reflection, Prayer, and Meditation

1. Take a moment to reflect on the burdens you carry. Write each of them down and ask God to carry them for you.

   _____

   _____

   _____

   _____

   _____

   _____

   _____

   _____

   _____

2. Thinking of the burdens you prayed about in the above question, which one is the most difficult to give to God? Write a request to God for you to trust Him with the burden.

   _____

   _____

   _____

   _____

   _____

   _____

   _____

3. Meditate, reflect, let go, and let God literally give you peace. Write down your gratitude for the peace that He is and will continue to give you if you accept it.

_____

_____

_____

_____

_____

_____

_____

YOUR RAY OF SONSHINE FOR TODAY

*It may be difficult at times
to stay on your journey
but God is your safe
and secure Guide.*

DAY 12

Thanks for the Memories

Some trust in chariots, and some in horses: but we will remember the name of the Lord our God.

Psalm 20:7

Memories are stored treasure that you can enjoy at any time.
Janice J. Browne

Good memories are little packages of joy wrapped in boxes of love and tied with bows of happiness.
Janice J. Browne

Never forget to remember.
Janice J. Browne

I remember as a little girl watching a program on television and at the end of the program the host would sing the song, "Thanks for the Memories." One day as I was reading the book of Psalms in my Bible, I read about David and his life of sadness and turmoil. I began to read how He thanked God for his protection and mercy. As I read the Psalms I instinctively started to thank God for the memories of how He had rescued me so many times from evil and physical danger. I started to sing to God "Thanks for the Memories."

David was a hunted man because of his gifts, talents, and exceptional abilities. He would one day sit on a royal throne and that did not make him a favorite of King Saul. Sometimes we have gifts, talents, and exceptional abilities. We have the possibility of sitting in very high places of noteworthiness. As a result of these possibilities we are sometimes hunted as David was by Saul. We are hunted by Saul's who will not give us a chance or go so far as to try and block our success.

These Saul's come in all forms and from all directions.

Like David, we love or admire them and wonder why they do not feel the same about us. We will help others to achieve their best selves and, yet it seems that that is not true for us. David wrote many Psalms lamenting and expressing those feelings. With love, admiration and great anguish, he wrote about his beloved King Saul and the pain of his hatred directed towards him.

But among what I call the "Pain Psalms" I found a lovely Psalm that still expressed David's thankfulness to God and recognition that God's mercy endures forever in spite of what was happening to him. "Praise ye the Lord. O give thanks unto the Lord; for He is good: for His mercy endureth forever" (Psalm 106:1).

Sometimes it may not be a person but a circumstance or a situation. As I go down memory lane I think of some of my situations that could have been fatal and stopped all that I was meant to do in this life.

On one occasion I was involved in a deadly accident where a drunken driver in another car hit a car behind me. The impact of that contact caused the drunken driver's car to fly up into the air landing on top of my car, causing my car to crash into the highway divider. By all accounts I should not be here to share this memory of God's mercy with you.

I remember thick black smoke and my car crashing and sliding down the concrete highway divider. Had the divider not been there I would have been in the middle of heavy traffic coming toward me from the opposite direction. I remember people hesitantly coming and looking inside my car. I remember getting into an ambulance and arriving at the hospital feeling very calm with the presence of God's surrounding me.

After being tested in every way possible a nurse came into my room with a curious expression on her face. The first words she spoke were "You have a great car!" I responded back by saying "No, I have a great God!" She smiled a big smile and said "I agree with you, you must be a believer. I could tell by your calmness when you arrived in the ambulance." It was determined that all I had was a broken nail on my left pinky finger. All I can say to God is "Thanks for the memories, your mercy endures forever!"

Time will not permit me to share the many memories I have which involve people, circumstances, and situations because it would take volumes. Memories of how I missed being struck by a train seconds before I crossed the tracks. The time I contracted a sickness I could have died from in Ethiopia, the hospital staff was amazed! Yes, I thank God for the memories of His protection, grace, and mercy that continues to endure forever.

I can imagine that you also have memories of protection and mercy through your pain and suffering. At this moment, whatever the channel the pain comes through it affects your emotions and your life as it did David. Today you may feel hunted, saddened and even angry. Read Psalm 107:1, "O give thanks unto the Lord, for he is good: for his mercy endureth forever." Relive the memories and think about the many ways God has protected you when it seemed hopeless and overwhelming. Never forget to remember.

Today, give thanks for His mercy endures forever just for you.

A Prayer for Today

Dear Father, thanks for the memories. Thank you that your mercy towards me endures forever! Amen.

Questions for Reflection, Prayer, and Meditation

1. How have you been hunted by a person or situation that seems to interfere with your dreams and goals?

   _____
   _____
   _____
   _____
   _____
   _____
   _____
   _____

2. Write a prayer asking God to help you overcome your sadness or anger about a person hunting you and interfering with your goals. Ask for God to help you move past it and for the strength to move forward.

   _____
   _____
   _____
   _____
   _____
   _____
   _____
   _____

3. Reflect and meditate on how God has given you grace and protection. Write it down.

_____

_____

_____

_____

_____

_____

_____

_____

YOUR RAY OF SONSHINE FOR TODAY

Let the good memories
fill your heart,
mind, and soul.

DAY 13
Singing Beauty

It is the beauty in God's heart that makes music.
Janice J. Browne

We can see with our heart.
Janice J. Browne

Our hearts can see what the eyes cannot.
Janice J. Browne

I thank God for allowing me to travel to so many wonderful places in the world. Each place has its own uniqueness and beauty. My travels have taken me from the back roads of Mississippi to the country side of Malawi and many places in between. The food, people, culture, and languages are always exhilarating for me. God has blessed me to make lifelong friends in every place I've been privileged to visit. God is good!

My husband and a group of his colleagues traveled to Southeast Asia to view the church work of digging wells, feeding centers, clinics, schools, and other projects to help the people of Southeast Asia. There is one place in particular that leaves me with a memory that I shall never forget, the place is Viet Nam. Before traveling there, I didn't know what to expect, how the people would react to strangers, and how it would look but I was excited to be going on this new venture.

Our first stop was at an elementary school. When we arrived, we saw the most beautiful little Vietnamese children. They had the biggest smiles on their faces. We could sense their excitement and I am sure that they could sense ours. When we walked into the room, the teacher gave them a signal and they stood in respect of us as visitors. Then the teacher told them to make a single file and to come to the front of the classroom so that they could sing for us.

Their little voices were so pure, innocent and sweet. They sang about the beauty of the day, bright sunshine, bumble bees on beautiful flowers and little birds. As they sang the songs they expressed it with their hands in beautiful, delicate, unified movement. At the end of the song we loudly and gratefully applauded their perfect performance.

The young teacher thanked us for coming and for our contribution to the school. She shared with us how much better life would be for those children. As a result of the education and training at the school they would not be beggars on the street or broom makers, the usual profession for the blind.

These children were blind from birth and would never be able to see. It was unbelievable they had never seen the trees, birds, bees, and the blue sky they sang so joyfully and compellingly about. My eyes filled with tears. I was sad they could not and would not ever see. Still, in their hearts and minds eye they saw and sang about God's beautiful creation. I will always remember hearing their sweet voices and their precious faces. They were singing beauty.

One day we are going to hear the most beautiful voice singing with great joy over us. *"He will joy over thee with singing"* (Zephaniah 3:17). He will be singing beauty over you!

A Prayer for Today

Dear Father, thank you for those children who saw your creation with their hearts and were able to sing about it. Help me to sing with faith about what I cannot see. Amen!

Questions for Reflection, Prayer, and Meditation

1. Sometimes we cannot see God with our naked eye, but we can feel His presence all around us. Ask God to give you more faith to believe that He exists even though you cannot see Him.

_____
_____
_____
_____
_____
_____
_____
_____
_____

2. Reflect and meditate on God's love for you through the everyday things you cannot always see with your eyes.

_____
_____
_____
_____
_____
_____
_____
_____
_____

3. Write a prayer asking God to give you faith to see Him with your heart.

_____
_____
_____
_____
_____
_____
_____

YOUR RAY OF SONSHINE FOR TODAY

*Keep a song
in your heart.*

DAY 14
Words of Wisdom

Wise words make the mind, soul, and spirit beautiful.
Janice J. Browne

Kind words build emotional safety for the mind.
Janice J. Browne

Wise words make the mind, soul, and spirit shine.
Janice J. Browne

Words are so important. Words can hurt, words can heal, words can bless, and words can kill. Words are very powerful. What we say and how we say it is truly noteworthy. We have heard the saying, "It's not what you say, it's how you say it." Well, it is both, what you say and how you say it.

This story begins with us receiving our boxes of clothing, household goods, and souvenirs from Ethiopia after waiting one long year. In the boxes, I saw my favorite pictures that my husband, Sweetie, purchased for me during one of our visits to Kenya. The pictures are brass colored with the appearance of burnish gold. They are so beautiful to the eyes, and when I look at them, a feeling of happiness comes over me. These pictures bring to my mind the text in Proverbs 25:11 where Solomon says, "A word fitly spoken is like apples of gold in pictures of silver." We want our words to shine like gold and to give people a feeling of happiness rather than feelings of hurt, sadness and pain.

We hold places of distinction and influence in our home with our spouse and children, in the church with the church members, on our jobs with our colleagues and in whatever we do or wherever we go.

What comes out of our mouth can determine the future of someone's path. Our words can make or break a person or a relationship. Some people will confide in us their hurts, remember Proverbs 11:13 that says, "A talebearer revealeth secrets: but he that is of a faithful spirit concealeth the matter." Do not reveal another's intimate feelings and thoughts they have trusted you with, be trustworthy and keep the secret.

Unfortunately, some people like to talk about others in a not so flattering way. Proverbs 26:22 reminds us, *"The words of a talebearer are as wounds, and they go down into the innermost parts of the belly."* Talebearers wound instead of healing.

Finally, Paul in Ephesians 4:29 tells us not to let any corrupt communication proceed out of our mouths, edify, enlighten and minister grace to the hearers. We cannot take unkind words back, but we can start fresh with our spouses, children, relatives, friends, colleagues and others who need to see Christ.

One day, we will hear the voice of God saying the words I long to hear, *"...Well done, thou good and faithful servant: thou hast been faithful over a few things: I will make thee ruler over many: enter thou into the joy of thy lord" (Matthew 25:21).* Let us remember we are royalty, children of the King, therefore, our words must always reflect Christ the King of the universe.

A Prayer for Today

Dearest Heavenly Father, please help me to be wise in my choice of words. Help me to use words that heal, bless, and lift you up. In the name of Jesus. Amen.

Questions for Reflection, Prayer, and Meditation

1. Reflect on an instance when words made a difference in your life. How did those words make you feel and how did they influence your life?

_____

_____

_____

_____

_____

_____

_____

_____

_____

2. When Jesus was on earth, His words were filled with hope and healing. Ask God to fill your words with hope and healing for yourself and others. Write it below.

_____

_____

_____

_____

_____

_____

_____

_____

_____

3. Meditate on God's love for you, then write some positive loving words to and about yourself right now.

_____

_____

_____

_____

_____

_____

YOUR RAY OF SONSHINE FOR TODAY

Speak good words
to yourself and others.

DAY 15

The Little Brown Bird

When thou passest through the waters, I will be with thee; and through the rivers, they shall not overflow thee: when thou walkest through the fire, thou shalt not be burned; neither shall the flame kindle upon thee.
Isaiah 43:2

Birds are God's way of singing songs to us each day.
Janice J. Browne

One lovely spring day my husband and I were enjoying breakfast on the veranda of our more than then 200-year-old home in Tennessee. As I recall it was one of the most beautiful, bright, sunny days I've ever experienced. The warm breeze flowed gently through the trees, butterflies flitted from flower to flower and the striped black and yellow bumblebees buzzed along with them as our dog, Mr. Browne, lazily bathed himself in the sun.

My attention turned to the many, beautiful, brightly colored birds that seemed to be enjoying their morning as much as I was mine. As I watched the birds, one bird became of special interest to me. A tiny, plain, brown bird in the midst of all of those brightly colored birds did not appear to be intimidated by the larger birds or by their beauty. The little brown bird flew from tree to tree, splashed in the birdbath, and ate the birdseed right along with the others.

I became so fascinated with the little bird, that I finally asked my pathfinder-nature-loving husband, "What kind of bird is that?" He looked at me with a smile and said, "Why, that's a sparrow." A Sparrow? I jumped to my feet in disbelief and said, "You mean that's the bird I sing about?" The last few words of the song came tenderly to my mind. "His eye is on the Sparrow and I know He watches me." It was at that moment that I again understood the love of God. I am that tiny, plain, brown bird!

Even my last name is Browne with an "e!"

"Are not two sparrows sold for a penny? Yet not one of them will fall to the ground outside your Father's care. And even the very hairs of your head are all numbered. So, don't be afraid; you are worth more than many sparrows" (Matthew 10:29-3, NIV).

How much more does He love you? You are of great value to God!

My eyes filled with tears and my heart was deeply moved. Imagine that! Not one sparrow falls without the notice of our heavenly Father. Not one of you experiences any difficulty in this life without His notice.

Sometimes we become afraid. Isaiah 41:10 says, *"Fear thou not; for I am with thee: be not dismayed; for I am thy God: I will strengthen thee; yea, I will help thee; yea, I will uphold thee with the right hand of my righteousness."* There may be times when your confidence is weak, and you think that someone is bigger and better, more beautiful or talented than you.

You may even ask yourself, "Does God love them more?" The answer is, no! God loves you. He loves you so much that He gave His only begotten son, John 3:16. You are special in His sight. God says to each of us, *"The Lord hath appeared of old unto me, saying, Yea, I have loved thee with an everlasting love: therefore, with lovingkindness have I drawn thee"* (Jeremiah 31:3). Are you feeling alone or forsaken? God tells us in Hebrews 13:5 *"...I will never leave thee nor forsake thee."* God is keeping watch over the little, brown birds, and remember He is keeping watch over you.

Prayer for Today

Heavenly Father, thank you for watching over those little brown Birds…and me—every minute of every day. Amen.

Questions for Reflection, Prayer, and Meditation

1. Do you feel uncomfortable or out of place in certain settings? Do you ever feel insecure or not good enough? Those feelings sometimes come into the mind, but you are good enough and smart enough. And you are especially loved by God for who you are. Write down the things that make you feel insecure or not good enough and why you may feel this way.

   _____

   _____

   _____

   _____

   _____

   _____

   _____

2. Write down your positive characteristics that God had given you.

   _____

   _____

   _____

   _____

   _____

3. Reflect and meditate on how you can use the positive characteristics God has given you. Maybe you should be writing a book, taking lessons of some kind, calling the sick, etc.

   _____

   _____

   _____

_____

_____

_____

_____

_____

_____

_____

YOUR RAY OF SONSHINE FOR TODAY

His eye is on the sparrow
and on you.

DAY 16
I Can Just Hear God Laughing

Imagine the laughter of God!
Janice J. Browne

Wow! I like your laugh, it's infectious!
Janice J. Browne

A gut-wrenching laugh is like a spring rain on the mind, soul, body, and spirit.
Janice J. Browne

A laugh deep from the belly is like a rain storm that washes the dust from the mind, soul, body, and spirit.
Janice J. Browne

Have you ever wondered if God laughs? I have, and you know what? I believe He does because He loves children and children can really cause you to laugh. On one occasion when the mothers brought their children to Jesus, the disciples tried to send them away, but Jesus stopped them and said, *"Suffer (permit)the little children to come unto me and forbid them not (don't stop them) for of such is the kingdom of heaven" (Mark 10:14, NASB).* That is one of my favorite texts. Sometimes, like the disciples, we become impatient, busy doing other things in life and we want to send the children away. God makes it plain in Psalm 127:3, *"Lo, children are an heritage of the Lord: and the fruit of the womb is His reward."* What a wonderful reward!!! He knows that we need them as much as they need us. Children take our minds away from the hardships and struggles of life. Jesus uses children as an example of how we should be in Matthew 18:2-3, *"And Jesus called a little child unto Him, and set him in the midst of them. And said, Verily I say unto you, Except ye be converted, and become as little children, ye shall not enter into the kingdom of heaven."*

When you stop to think about it, children are innocent, transparent, honest, and can be very humorous. God loves children and He must laugh, because children can say the funniest and most sincere things one could ever hear.

There is just no end to the love, joy and humor my nieces and nephews bring to my heart. Sometimes, when I think about the humorous and innocent things they have said, I am filled with laugher. I believe God laughs with me. Case in point, we adults were in what we considered a deep theological debate, and after some time my brother-in-law, Muyiwa said, "I just don't see it!" Kemi, my eldest niece in a very quizzical manner looked up at her dad and said in the most concerned and innocent tone, "Daddy do you need glasses?" God and we all laughed.

As adults sometimes when we find something hard to believe we may respond with the cliché, "I wasn't born yesterday." On another occasion, my sister Rosalind overheard my niece Kemi trying to convince my nephew Stephen about her point to which Stephen her younger brother replied. "Look Kemi, I wasn't born tomorrow!" Born tomorrow! I wonder if God laughed as much as their mother and I did when she shared it with me?

Of course, I must share with you another favorite humorous moment. One evening when my sister-in-law, Joyce, and my brother Washington II, shared the news that Sweetie had been elected president, their son whom we affectionately call Trey, with the earnestness of a seven-year-old asked, "Is he President of the United States?" We all laughed and let him know his uncle was elected to be president of a conference of churches.

Finally, let me share one last humorous moment. One day I was in the kitchen preparing a salmon salad for some guests when Andrew, the youngest of my nieces and nephews, the son of Stephanie and Gil, came running into the kitchen. He frowned, covered his nose and said, "Tati Mimi that fish stinks!!! Do you think he had an accident in his pants?!!" I laughed and laughed and laughed. I think God joined in that laugh with me.

It is good to laugh Proverbs 17:22 says, *"A merry heart doeth good like a medicine: but a broken spirit drieth the bones."* Laughter is good for our mind, soul, body, and spirit. Dr. Lee Berk of the Loma Linda University School of Medicine in his research on laughter reported that even anticipating laugher has a positive effect upon the body. We have all heard the cliché, "I laughed until I cried." Laughter just makes us feel better. That is why I firmly believe God gave us children and laugher.

We are children of God. Roman 8:16 says, *"The Spirit itself beareth witness with our spirit, that we are the children of God:"* Jesus Christ has claimed us as His children; all we need to do is accept our role. Paul says in Galatians 3:26, *"For ye are all the children of God by faith in Christ Jesus."* Become as a little child, keep a merry heart and learn to laugh, it's good for you!!!

A Prayer for Today

Father, thank you for children and the laughter they bring to my heart. Help me to laugh more. In the name of Jesus. Amen.

Questions for Reflection, Prayer, and Meditation

1. Reflect for a moment and think of the funniest thing that you can think of and laugh out loud...real loud!

    _____
    _____
    _____
    _____
    _____
    _____
    _____
    _____
    _____

2. At this moment I want you to stop and just smile, then go the mirror, look at yourself and smile again. It will feel great!

    _____
    _____
    _____
    _____
    _____
    _____
    _____
    _____
    _____

3. Ready a funny story. Talk to a child. Watch a wholesome funny movie and laugh. Guess what? There are some funny stories in the Bible too. Look for one and laugh, laugh, laugh!

    _____
    _____
    _____
    _____
    _____

YOUR RAY OF SONSHINE FOR TODAY

Enjoy lots of laughter today.

DAY 17

Fruit over Nuts

When you plant seeds of love, joy, peace, and contentment they will spring up in your life.
Janice J. Browne

I love nuts. They come in all colors, shapes, and sizes.
Janice J. Browne

After almost one year of living with our wonderful family and re-bonding after being away for a number of years in Ethiopia, God directed us to the place He intended to be our home. I was so excited about our new house.

So many preparations…pack the accumulation of personal belongings at my sister Rosalind and her family's home, call the realtor one more time to be sure all is in place, call the storage manager and oh, don't forget to schedule the closing a day early because I'm traveling to a retreat where I'll be the keynote speaker for the weekend. Whew! Somehow, we managed to get it all done.

During the course of the weekend I spent each spare moment between the messages thinking about where I was to live, whether our neighbors would be friendly, if they would welcome us to the neighborhood and on and on and on. Then suddenly a great idea popped into my mind!

I know what I will do; I will witness to the whole neighborhood! I decided on a definite plan of action. First, I would go to each house with a bowl of fruit (with Sweetie in tow), introduce myself, and send flyers to each person telling them when the next religious meeting or Bible Seminar would occur. Then I would start Bible Study meetings and have a Christmas open house with a religious church flavor, whatever that is. On and on I went again.

Then, more plans popped into my head. I know, I will also get involved in the neighborhood association and make sure they know I cannot have meetings on my day of worship -- you know letting them know that I was a religious person. Witness, witness, witness. Whew! I was making myself tired.

One day my husband, Sweetie said to me, "Slow down, take it one step at a time, we can just casually meet, greet and start the witnessing by being good neighbors." I did not quite see his point. Aren't we sent here to the neighborhood for a purpose? Aren't we supposed to let our light shine before men? Where was his evangelistic spirit? Maybe I need to witness to him about this big opportunity to win the neighborhood for Christ! I was enthusiastic about this new endeavor!

Then it happened. One Sunday my brother Grayland came to visit. During his visit, we decided to go to a beautiful farm. There it was in route, a big, bright sign that read, "God prefers the Fruit of the Spirit over religious nuts! Religious nuts? I laughed when I thought about me and my plans. Was I being a religious nut? The answer was definitely, yes!

A few days later as I was looking out of my dining room window, I saw people in the middle of the day all dressed in black going in and out of the neighbor's house, someone had died. I called Sweetie, told Him what I saw, and asked him what he thought I should do? In his usual calm, agreeable way he said, "Do whatever you feel you should do." I hung up the telephone, and prayed for guidance from the Holy Spirit. Galatians 5:22-23 came to my mind, *"But the fruit of the Spirit is love, joy, peace, longsuffering, gentleness, goodness, faith. Meekness, temperance: against such there is no law."*

There was the answer. Instead of being a religious nut, I could share the

89

fruit of the Spirit in their time of need, which is what I was able to do by showing them love, kindness and being there for them. God's word says, *"And the second is like unto it, Thou shalt love they neighbour as thyself"* (Matthew 22:39). I came to realize it is not about my religion, but rather about the witness of the love of God. Ecclesiastes 3:1 tells us, *"To every thing there is a season, and a time to every purpose under the heaven:"* This was the time to comfort, love and show compassion.

Think about it. Are you a religious nut or do you share the fruit of the Spirit? God prefers the fruit of the Spirit over religious nuts.

A Prayer for Today

Heavenly Father, help us to share with others the fruit of the Spirit. Amen.

Questions for Reflection, Prayer, and Meditation

1. Write down each fruit of the Spirit, and as you write, reflect and mediate on each one. What do they mean to you?

   _____

   _____

   _____

   _____

   _____

   _____

   _____

2. Think of an instance when you had the perfect opportunity to share God's love instead of a sermon but didn't. How could you have acted differently?

   _____

   _____

   _____

   _____

   _____

_____
_____
_____

3. In what ways can you share the fruit of the Spirit with others?

_____
_____
_____
_____
_____
_____
_____
_____
_____

YOUR RAY OF SONSHINE FOR TODAY

Plant a seed of love today.

DAY 18
The Forgotten Prayer

What a comfort there is in knowing that when we have forgotten our prayers, they are still lingering in the ears and heart of God.
Janice J. Browne

How quickly we forget. How long God remembers.
Janice J. Browne

t is so amazing to me that God takes care of each of us here on this earth. He knows each of us by name and the number of every strand of hair on our heads. Matthew 10:30 reads, *"But the very hairs of your head are all numbered."* Imagine that! He knows everything about us!!

I am further amazed when I think of all the requests we make in our prayers. Mine alone could probably keep the Maker rather busy. He never forgets our requests and answers them all according to His own time and will.

God has given us permission to ask, believe, and receive. We read in Matthew 7:7-8, *"Ask, and it shall be given you; seek, and ye shall find; knock, and it shall be open unto you: For every one that asketh receiveth: and he that seeketh findeth: and to him that knocketh it shall be opened."*

On her 16th birthday a young girl's parents gave her the traditional family birthday party. It was a wonderful and exciting time. It was the party where each child must announce to the family their future plans instead of just making a birthday wish and blowing out the candles. The family was pleasantly surprised when the birthday girl stated that her prayer was to be a missionary. No one in the family nor anyone they knew had ever been a missionary. They were pleased with the prayer request and together petitioned God to lead and guide her.

Years passed, and she forgot all about the prayer. The young girl grew up, married, attended school and became a professional. As time continued, God blessed her in so many ways. Life was wonderful. However, as is the case in life, there were happy and tragic times such as the loss of a son at birth. But because she loved and trusted God with her whole heart she was comforted by His promise, *"For the Lord himself will come down from heaven, with a loud command, with the voice of the archangel and with the trumpet call of God, and the dead in Christ will rise first. After that, we who are still alive and are left will be caught up together with them in the clouds to meet the Lord in the air. And so, we will be with the Lord forever"* 1 *Thessalonians 4:16-17*, NIV*)*. Her heart was comforted by these words.

One evening she and her father was sitting and talking together when the telephone rang, and guess who it was? It was a caller on the line asking her husband if they would serve as missionaries. She could not believe her ears! Serves as missionaries? What a dream come true! What a joy! Even though she did not realize it at the time, the prayer she prayed years ago as a teenager was answered.

I was that young girl who, so many years before had asked God to allow me to serve Him as a missionary. I did not remember my prayer until my sister Stephanie reminded me of my 16th birthday party and how they prayed for me to become a missionary.

Sometimes when we pray, and we do not get an answer right away or for many years, we think God has forgotten. God never forgets. He promises that he will never forget us in Isaiah 49:15 where He asks and answers the question, "Can a woman forget her sucking child, that she should not have compassion on the son of her womb? yea, they may forget, yet will I not forget thee." Oh, what a loving, kind and compassionate God we serve.

At this moment, right now, if you are praying for something and have been praying for a very long time do not get discouraged, do not give up. Forget about the prayer and leave it with God. David tells us in Psalm 37:5, *"Commit your way to the Lord; trust also in Him; And He shall bring it to pass."* Give it to Him, trust Him with it and when He knows you are ready, He will make it happen if it is in your best interests and for His glory.

Sometimes we become impatient and foolishly run ahead of God to our own detriment and sorrow. *"Wait on the Lord: be of good courage, and He shall strengthen thine heart: wait, I say, on the Lord" (Psalm 27:14).*

It is better to wait than to have our own plan apart from God.

God answered my forgotten prayer and He will answer yours. Be faithful, patient and wait. Isaiah 64:4 says, *"For since the beginning of the world men have not heard, nor perceived by the ear, neither hath the eye seen, O God, beside thee, what he hath prepared for him that waiteth for him."*

A Prayer for Today

Heavenly Father thank you for hearing and answering my prayers. Help me to pray with faith and patience. May your will be done in my life. Amen.

Questions for Reflection, Prayer, and Meditation

1. Have you been praying for something for a very long time and have not received it? Meditate on the thought that God is saying yes, no, or wait a little longer. He never forgets your prayer. Write a prayer for it and leave it with God.

   _____

   _____

   _____

   _____

   _____

   _____

_____
_____

2. Sometimes we want what we want, but God knows that is not the best for us. Ask God to help you with His insight into your prayer. Ask Him to reveal His will to you.

_____
_____
_____
_____
_____
_____
_____
_____
_____

3. Write a prayer that is reflective of your desire to have patience and trust in the fact that God knows what He is doing. Ask for strength to wait.

_____
_____
_____
_____
_____
_____
_____
_____
_____

YOUR RAY OF SONSHINE FOR TODAY

Pray and wait.

DAY 19

Plot or Plan?

*Call unto me, and I will answer thee, and show thee great and
mighty things, which thou knowest not,*
Jeremiah 33:3

*For I know the thoughts I think towards you, saith the Lord,
thoughts of peace, and not of evil, to give you an expected end.*
Jeremiah 29:11

*Some of the goals written by God in His life plan for you are hope, a good future, and
success.*
Janice J. Browne

In God's eyes you are a success!
Janice J. Browne

One of my favorite pastimes while travelling is reading church signs. They can be humorous, clever and sometimes thought provoking. One such sign that caused me to think about this reading, "Satan has a plot, but God has a plan."

As I continued to ponder, I decided to look up the word "plot." It means a secret plan that is intended to undermine a person or government. How awful. Think about it, Satan wants to undermine us and overthrow the kingdom of heaven. He wants to destroy any good plan God has for you and me. 1 Peter 5:8 reminds us, *"Be sober, be vigilant; because your adversary the devil, as a roaring lion, walketh about, seeking whom he may devour."*

For a moment, I felt shaken by the thought but remembered the promises of God in His Holy Word. In Jeremiah 29:11 we read the inspiring words of God, *"For I know the plans I have for you, declares the Lord, plans to prosper you and not to harm you, plans to give you hope and a future."* What a precious thought! Hope and a future! God's plans are designed to help you. His plans were not put together yesterday or last week. Before you were born He had a plan in place for you just as he did the Prophet Jeremiah. God says in Jeremiah 1:5, *"Before I formed thee in the belly I knew thee; and before thou camest forth out of the womb I sanctified thee…"*

When you feel that your plans are failing, remember Psalm 27:14, *"Wait on the Lord: be of good courage, and He shall strengthen thine heart: wait, I say, on the Lord."* Be assured that whatever He has started in you will be completed. Philippians 1:6 says, *"Being confident of this very thing, that He which hath begun a good work in you will perform it until the day of Jesus Christ:"*

Give your dreams, visions and desires to God. If you have a talent or a gift that God has given you, keep it polished. Practice and prepare so that when the time comes to use it, you will be ready. Above all, put God first. *"Delight thyself also in the Lord: and He shall give thee the desires of thine heart"* (Psalm 37:4).

Do you feel that you do not have the wisdom to do a good job? Jeremiah 33:3 says, *"Call unto me, and I will answer thee, and show thee great and might things, which thou knowest not."* He can give you all of the knowledge and the expertise to perform the task He has set before you. I am a living witness to that fact; He is helping me at this very moment to write His words of encouragement to you.

He can even mend broken dreams and visions. It is never too late to live your dream or vision. *"Trust in the Lord with all thine heart; and lean not unto thine own understanding. In all thy ways acknowledge Him, and He shall direct thy paths"* (Proverbs 3:5, 6).

Do not become discouraged when your plans do not turn out the way you thought they should. *"And we know that all things work together for good to them that love God, to them who are the called according to his purpose"* (Romans 8:28).

I went to a job interview and did so well that at the end of the interview the persons who interviewed me gave me a standing ovation. Still, I did not get the job. I was crushed. I later found out that a church member prevented me from getting the job. I was crushed again. A few days later a friend told me of a job he thought was perfect for me.

Grudgingly I went to the interview, and wouldn't you know it I got the job. It was the best job I have ever had! The job afforded me the opportunity to work with the then Surgeon General of the United States. It also provided me with volunteer subjects for my doctoral dissertation. Furthermore, I received one of the highest humanitarian awards from the Governor of Tennessee for my work in Suicide Prevention, appeared on the cover of a magazine and was featured on television and world radio.

Was God's plan not better? Had I gotten the previous job, I would never have had such great experiences. Sometimes what is meant for evil, God means for good. My dad always told me that, "Sometimes when you think things are at their worst and working against you, they are working positively for you and on your best behalf." When things do not go as you plan remember, Satan may have a plot, but God has a plan.

A Prayer for Today

Father, thank you for the plans you have for my life. Help me to live within your will.
Amen!

Questions for Reflection, Prayer, and Meditation

1. Reflect on a time in your life when something was done for evil, but God turned it into something good? Write the situation down and write a prayer of gratitude for God foiling the plot of Satan.

    _____

    _____

    _____

    _____

    _____

    _____

    _____

    _____

    _____

2. Meditate for a moment. If you are experiencing a plot right now in your life write a prayer asking God to overthrow the plot, to keep you fearless, and to give you a great ending.

    _____

    _____

    _____

    _____

    _____

    _____

    _____

    _____

    _____

3. If you had just one opportunity to share God's miraculous power over the devil, which Bible story would you use? Discuss the significance of that story in your own life.

    _____

    _____

    _____

    _____

_____

_____

_____

_____

_____

_____

_____

YOUR RAY OF SONSHINE FOR TODAY

Give all of your plans
to God.

DAY 20
Chipped, Battered, and Broken

Welcome to the chipped, battered, and broken club.
Your membership includes passion and determination.
Janice J. Browne

We get chipped, battered, and broken in this life but we can still be whole.
Janice J. Browne

I was invited to speak at a college for an Appreciation Tea given in honor of graduating seniors and dormitory deans. The theme I was given to speak on was, "If Tea Cups Could Talk." Umm, I thought to myself, what could I say that would be just what they need to hear. As usual, I went excitedly to Sweetie and asked him about his thoughts on teacups (after all he is a preacher!). He began to remind me of the qualities of teacups.

Teacups are beautiful, light and fragile. Though they are light, and fragile, they can hold very hot water. We are also like teacups; we are fragile but sometimes have to handle very hot situations. It is during those times that we can trust God for the strength that He has promised, *"When you pass through the waters, I will be with you; and when you pass through the rivers, they will not sweep over you. When you walk through the fire, you will not be burned; the flames will not set you ablaze" (Isaiah 43:2, NIV).* God keeps His promises. You will survive.

Sometimes hot situations make us fearful and dismayed, we become weak and feel that we will not make it. God tells us in Isaiah 41:10, *"Fear thou not: for I am with thee: be not dismayed; for I am thy God: I will strengthen thee; yea, I will help thee; yea, I will uphold thee with the right hand of my righteousness."* I know His promises are true. God will strengthen you just as He has strengthened me.

As I continued to think about teacups, I thought about my beautiful Ethiopian dishes that arrived with our cargo from Ethiopia. They are green, red, and yellow, the colors of the Ethiopian flag, and beautiful brown Ethiopian faces with large Ethiopian eyes encircle each dish. To my amazement, most of the dishes arrived unbroken, truly a miracle. To my disappointment though, a few of the dishes were chipped, cracked or broken.

I was grateful for the ones that arrived undamaged, but all I could think about was the damaged ones and how to get them replaced. Should I ask my friend Curdell to send me replacements? Well, that did not make a lot of sense, because they would have to be shipped again and who could guarantee the same thing wouldn't happen?

Then it happened! Surprisingly, I received an e-mail that my friend Yazumnesh was coming to the US for her son's graduation and would visit with us. I was so excited about seeing her. I knew I could ask her to bring the replacement dishes. Then I would have my perfect set again. I was overjoyed!

I just knew my husband would be overjoyed also. Instead, his response surprised me. He said, "The ones that are broken, I can glue together for you, and you will never be able to tell that they were broken. The ones that are chipped can be used." My husband went on to say, "The brokenness and the chips show that the dishes have been through something." Wow! What a thought! I couldn't stop thinking about his words, "been through something."

Sometimes we are broken, battered and chipped— we've all been through something. As you read this meditation today, you might be experiencing a broken heart or a chipped spirit. He can heal your hurt and your heart. The promise in Psalm 147:3 reads, *"He healeth the broken in heart, and bindeth up their wounds."*

I have good news for you the Master Potter can put you back together again. Isaiah 64:8 reads *"But now, O Lord, thou art our father; we are the clay, and thou our potter; and we all are the work of thy hand."* His hand makes our brokenness perfect. God restores. Even though we may be battered or chipped, we are still of worth and value to our Father and to others.

A Prayer for Today

Father, I feel battered, chipped, and sometimes broken. I ask you to put me back together again as only you can. In the name of Jesus. Amen.

Questions for Reflection, Prayer, and Meditation

1. Life certainly has a way of battering us when we least expect it. Write an experience that battered you.

_____
_____
_____
_____
_____
_____
_____
_____
_____

2. Record your favorite scripture you refer to when you feel battered and the reason you cling to those words?

_____
_____
_____
_____
_____
_____
_____
_____

3. Are you holding on to an emotion, relationship or past experience that may be hindering your spiritual growth? Write a short prayer asking God to help you release it.

_____

_____

_____

_____

_____

_____

_____

_____

_____

YOUR RAY OF SONSHINE FOR TODAY

At this very moment
open yourself up to healing.

DAY 21
Hats and Crowns

Henceforth there is laid up for me a crown of righteousness, which the Lord, the righteous judge, shall give me at that day: and not to me only, but unto all them also that love his appearing.
2 Timothy 4:8

You are royalty, so wear your crown with dignity.
Janice J. Browne

Your Highness, your chariot of love and crown of beauty awaits you!
Janice J. Browne

"Oh, that one is gorgeous on you", my mother said as I tried on the glittering pearly hat. "I'm going to get that one for you." "No mother," I replied, "it's too expensive!" She did not respond to me but instead told the milliner to box it up and that we would carry it with us. I enjoy wearing hats and I am sure one of the reasons I wear them is because I admire my mother who has worn them since I can remember They make me feel feminine, and for me it is my special attire as I attend church.

That hat is one of my favorites. I wear it every chance I get. I call it my "queen hat" or "my crown." Sweetie calls me the "Queen of Sheba" when I wear it. The hat glitters and is shaped in the form of a turban. It has tiny iridescent white and gold pearls wrapped completely around it with rhinestones around the edges. It shines just like a crown and reminds me of the thought that one day we will wear crowns in heaven. There is a deeper meaning that I find in that hat. It reminds me of heaven and all of the unimaginable beauty that awaits me and those who look forward to heaven. The bible tells us in 1 Corinthians 2:9. *"But as it is written, Eye hath not seen, nor ear heard, neither have entered into the heart of man, the things which God hath prepared for them that love him."*

I have purposed in my heart that everything I do, say and wear must reflect heaven. Let me share with you how heaven is reflected to me in that hat. As I look at the swirling pearls at the top of the hat, I think about Orion, a galaxy of stars naked to the human eye. In Job 38:31, God asks Job the question, *"Canst thou bind the sweet influence of Pleiades, or loose the bands of Orion?"* Who but the creator could have put the clusters of stars in space?

I try to imagine each time I wear my hat that the pearls represent the pearly gates. As I continue to gaze upon the hat, the white pearls draw my mind to the pearly gates described in Revelation 21:21 that says, *"And the twelve gates were twelve pearls: every several gate was of one pearl."* In addition, the gold pearls on the hat remind me of the completion of that same verse "and the street of the city was pure gold, as it were transparent glass." Imagine that! Pearly gates and streets of gold!

Wait! There is more! When trials and tribulations come into our life, if we are faithful to God, He promises us a crown of life in Revelation 2:10 we read the promise, *"...be thou faithful unto death, and I will give thee a crown of life."* How marvelous! What a wonderful promise. Life eternal from the life-giver! *"And God shall wipe away all tears from their eyes; and there shall be no more death, neither sorrow, nor crying, neither shall there be any more pain: for the former things are passed away"* (Revelation 21:4).

Saying good-bye be it by death or travel is difficult, but in heaven, there will be no more separation by death or geography. Revelation 21:1 reads, *"And I saw a new heaven and a new earth: for the first heaven and the first earth were passed away; and there was no more sea."*

The sea separates continents and people. No more separation, no more goodbyes or farewells. I will see Jonathan, our infant son, Daddy my beloved and loving Father, grandparents, aunts, uncles, a mother-in-law, my siblings Cynthia and Grayland. I am sure there are people you long to see also. You will see them because God has made a promise that we will meet again, if we are faithful.

Yes, I can imagine heaven in an earthly hat that does not compare to heaven. I thank God for a godly mother who helped me to see heaven in the hat that she purchased for me. Until Jesus comes, I will be practicing for my heavenly crown.

Heaven! What a joy to think of Heaven.

A Prayer for Today

Dear Heavenly Father, help me to be all that you want me to be so that I may see you face to face and wear a crown that will be placed upon my head by your own hands. Amen.

Questions for Reflection, Prayer, and Meditation

1. Are you looking forward to the blessing of our Savior's return? What are you doing to get ready for it? Write it down.

   _____

   _____

   _____

   _____

   _____

   _____

   _____

   _____

2. Read about Heaven in Revelation 22 and meditate on what it will be like. Write it in detail, with color.

   _____

   _____

   _____

_____
_____
_____
_____
_____
_____
_____

3. Write the names of people you would love to see in heaven with you. Think of one individual who may be in danger of missing out on heaven and write a prayer on behalf of that person.

_____
_____
_____
_____
_____
_____
_____
_____
_____

YOUR RAY OF SONSHINE FOR TODAY

You are very special.
All of heaven is waiting
for you.

DAY 22

The Open Door

The LORD is my light and my salvation; whom shall I fear? The LORD is the strength of my life; of whom shall I be afraid?
Psalm 27:1

Yea, though I walk through the valley of the shadow of death, I will fear no evil: for thou art with me; thy rod and thy staff they comfort me.
Psalm 23:4

Your only safety is in God the greatest protector.
Janice J. Browne

We had just made the long journey back to our home in Nashville, Tennessee. We were exhausted and could not get into bed fast enough. We said our prayers, told each other of our love for the other and fell asleep. Oh, the bed felt so wonderful after being in a car for hours and hours.

To our surprise and little did we know until the next morning when Sweetie was leaving for his office, that all of the doors including the garage doors were left opened or unlocked all night. As we discussed it, we thanked God for His wonderful love and protection. I told my husband that I was really thankful to God for leading us to a "safe" neighborhood.

As I continued to think about the goodness of God and the "safe" neighborhood, the thought came to my mind that it was not the safety of the neighborhood that protected us. Crimes can occur at any time in any neighborhood, no matter how safe it seems. It was the protection and goodness of God that kept us safe from hurt, harm, and danger. He guarded those open doors. He sends His angels to protect us. Psalm 34:7 says, *"The angel of the LORD encampeth round about them that fear Him, and delivereth them."*

As I thought about the doors being guarded, I remembered when we lived in Ethiopia and how the guards protected the compound from intruders. On our compound were fifteen other families, an elementary school, daycare center, book press and church. There was a large brick wall in front of the compound with two guards stationed there 24 hours each day seven days a week.

No one was allowed to come in without proper identification. Sometimes even if they had identification, if they were not familiar or seemed unsavory the guards would contact the persons they came to visit. Every hour on the hour after sunset the guards would walk around the compound with long black shiny guns (that they would not hesitate to use) to keep people out who might try to climb the back fence with criminal intent.

I had great love and respect for those guards and the difficult work they performed. We always remembered them at meal times and holidays. They were protective and kind to us. There was no end to our appreciation for them but there is no protection like the protection of our Father, Jesus, the Holy Spirit and the angels. Psalm 91:11 reads, "For He shall give His angels charge over thee, to keep thee in all thy ways." Psalms 91:7 says, "A thousand shall fall at thy side, and ten thousand at thy right hand; but it shall not come nigh thee." He will not allow a thief or robber to come near you.

God loves us and cares about us. In Jeremiah 31:3, He says, *"...I have loved thee with an everlasting love."* He protects, leads, guides and directs us. *"I will instruct thee and teach thee in the way which thou shalt go: I will guide thee with mine eye" (Psalm 32:8).* What powerful eyes they are, and they are always on us to protect and shield us. That is how great His love is for you and for me.

I remember when I was in elementary school the boys would write the name of the one they loved that day on their hands in black ink. We called it puppy love, love that would last only as long as the ink.

God loves us so much that He has put our names on His hands not in ink but with nails. He says in Isaiah 49:16 *"Behold, (look) I have graven thee upon the palms of my hands; thy walls are continually before me."* That is not puppy love that is real love. His precious hands forever bear nail marks just for us. *"Greater love hath no man than this, that a man lay down his life for his friends"* (John 15:13). We are not only his children, we are His friends. This friend has died to protect us.

One day and I believe soon, we will be in a place where we will not be concerned with unlocked doors, security systems, police or guards. We will have no need for gated communities. That place is called heaven— a place of safety, security, and comfort. Jesus will be there, and we will be safe forevermore!

A Prayer for Today

Father, thank you for your love and protection over me day and night. I look forward to Heaven where you, my protector, will be the center of my peace and safety. In the precious name of Jesus. Amen.

Questions for Reflection, Prayer, and Meditation

1. You may be walking through the valley of the shadow of death because of a diagnosis, divorce, or the death of a loved one, but be assured that your Shepherd is with you in that valley and will bring you through. Meditate on this and write your words of reflection on the story.

_____

_____

_____

_____

_____

_____

_____

_____

2. You have heard the saying, "Bad things even happen to good people." Write the Bible promise, Proverbs 3:5-6. What does this text of scripture say about trust? Write other promises that may encourage you in these tough times in your life.

_____

_____

_____

_____

_____

_____

_____

_____

_____

3. What does Psalm 91:11 personally mean to you?

_____

_____

_____

_____

_____

_____

_____

_____

_____

YOUR RAY OF SONSHINE FOR TODAY

*You are safe
in the arms of Jesus.*

DAY 23

Promises

When love is in the air our mind, soul, and spirit sparkle.
Janice J. Browne

Love brightens the dark places in our hearts and lives.
Janice J. Browne

A promise is like a beautiful diamond wrapped up in hope.
Janice J. Browne

It was a beautiful summer day. Everything seemed to sparkle. Seemingly the sun shone brighter, the trees were taller, and the flowers looked more colorful than ever before. I felt like a princess in a storybook as I walked down the aisle arm in arm with my beloved Father. I could feel the love of my handsome husband-to-be as he stood tall in his black tuxedo. A wedding party of friends, relative and onlookers from around the world watched as we declared our love to God and each other.

Then came the question from Pastor Bradford, "Do you promise to love, cherish, honor and obey?" It was not the first time we had thought of that question. We frequently discussed the promise as we anticipated our future.

We fasted, prayed, attended marital counseling and felt impressed by the Holy Spirit that God was leading us. Therefore, without hesitation we made that promise to each other on that day knowing what it meant, and with the help of God to this day are staying true to it.

Only God can help us to love for He is love. *"Beloved, let us love one another: for love is of God; and everyone that loveth is born of God, and knoweth God. He that loveth not knoweth not God; for God is love" (1 John 4:7-8).* God's grace is sufficient to help us honor, cherish, and obey each other. God's grace is sufficient to help us in every way and in our weakest moments in life. *"And he said unto me, My grace is sufficient for thee: for my strength is made perfect in weakness" (2 Corinthians 12:9).*

Promises give us hope, something to look forward to and are usually positive with an attached benefit. We make promises to call, visit and sometimes promise gifts to our children for holidays and birthdays. It is always our intention to fulfill these promises, but because we are human, and life is unpredictable, we may not always be able to keep those promises.

Perhaps you broke a promise to someone or someone broke a promise to you. It may have happened more than once and when promises are continually broken, it is difficult to trust. We all break promises, but there is one who never breaks a promise to us, His name is Jesus. The one we can trust and always depend on.

You may have broken or experienced broken promises, and at this moment, you need to hear promises that will never be broken. God has a promise for every need we experience in life. *"For all the promises of God in him are yea, and in him Amen, unto the glory of God by us" (2 Corinthians 1:20).*

Take hold of the promises God has made to you and remember as you take hold of them they will never be broken. He also promises that He is always with you. *"He hath said, I will never leave thee, nor forsake thee" (Hebrews 13:5).* You are never alone. Are you experiencing a broken promise, heart or spirit? Do you need comfort? God says in John 14:18, *"I will not leave you comfortless: I will come to you."*

Sometimes the battles, sorrows and trials of life seem to come in multitudes.

The same promise given to Judah, Jerusalem, and King Jehoshaphat applies to us, *"And He said, Harken you, all Judah, and ye inhabitants of Jerusalem, and thou King Jehoshaphat, Thus saith the Lord unto you, Be not afraid not dismayed by reason of this great multitude; for the battle is not yours, but God's"* (2 Chronicles 20:15).

Is there a need for something in your life? *"But seek ye first the kingdom of God, and His righteousness; and all these things shall be added unto you"* (Matthew 6:33). Put God first and the rest will come, He promised. If you are facing sickness pray these words they are for you. *"Heal me, O LORD, and I shall be healed; save me, and I shall be saved: for thou art my praise"* (Jeremiah 17:14). Start praising Him for your healing now!

Trust Him. We have all experienced death close to us or from a distance. The experience is one of the most difficult and causes us to cry tears of pain and anguish but remember this promise, *"For his anger endureth but a moment; in his favor is life: weeping may endure for a night, but joy cometh in the morning"* (Psalm 30:5). Oh yes, the morning is coming and there will be no more tears. *"And God shall wipe away all tears from their eyes; and there shall be no more death, neither sorrow, nor crying, neither shall there be any more pain: for the former things are passed away"* (Revelation 21:4).

Many things will happen in life, changes will take place, people will come and go, but the words of this passage are the most comforting. *"Heaven and earth shall pass away: but my words shall not pass away"* (Mark 13:31).

Finally, the most wonderful promise of all is that Christ has promised to come and get us with a present for us. *"Behold I am coming soon my reward with me (Rev 22:13-14)."* He repeats it again in Revelation 22:20, *"Surely I come quickly"*—He promises.

A Prayer for Today

Dear Father, thank you for your promises. Give us faith to take hold of every promise you have given to us. Amen.

Questions for Reflection, Prayer, and Meditation

1. Think of a promise that you broke to a loved one and describe the effect(s) it had on that person. What did you do to rebuild that person's trust?

   _____
   _____
   _____
   _____
   _____
   _____
   _____
   _____
   _____

2. Of the 3,600 promises in the Bible, list one that you hold dear in your heart. What makes this promise so special to you?

   _____
   _____
   _____
   _____
   _____
   _____
   _____
   _____

3. What promises are you willing to make to God?

   _____
   _____
   _____
   _____
   _____
   _____
   _____

YOUR RAY OF SONSHINE FOR TODAY

*Let go and let God
love you.*

DAY 24

You May Enter

Every door is not an opportunity. Some doors are traps.
Janice J. Browne

Pray for obedience and direction to enter safe doors of opportunity.
Janice J. Browne

I was so excited! It was my first trip abroad alone. My parents had taken my siblings and me abroad in times past but this time I traveled on my own just God and me.

As an instructor at a college, I was awarded a fellowship to study abroad in any country of my choosing. I chose Nigeria. Why? I do not know; possibly, it was having Nigerian students in my class or perhaps it was just a sense of adventure and curiosity about the country. Whatever the reason, I was so thankful that God had heard my prayer to travel the world, and this was yet another place to add to my list of journeys.

After eighteen hours of travel the plane began it's decent; my heart thumped with excitement and anticipation. The flight attendants quickly took their seats and the pilot made the announcement that within a few short minutes we would be landing in Lagos. Sure enough within what seemed like an hour but was only 30 minutes, I was off the plane and standing in a long line with people speaking different dialects, sweltering heat and cabbies waiting to transport us to our various destinations. The line seemed endless, and the stifling heat, along with people trying to get into the country, was not the most exciting beginning. After standing in the line for what seemed like eternity but was only about ten minutes, something interesting happened. A tall slender young man came toward me and with a kind face and friendly voice said, "Follow me." I really did not know if I should follow him, but a voice inside said, "obey him." As I passed the people in the long line I thought to myself, I have all of my documents, what else could they want? I prayed a short prayer, "God be with me." The young man took me straight to front of the line.

When we got to the front of the line a stern looking custom's officer looked at me, my passport and accompanying documents. After another eternity of about five minutes, the once stern officer smiled and said, "You may enter."

YOU MAY ENTER! Oh, such lovely words to my ears. You may enter. I was very happy that I met all of the regulations that were necessary to enter through the gate into the country. How could this be? It just reassured me that God had heard my prayer and was taking care of me.

Someday soon, I hope to take another journey, a heavenly journey. I invite you to prepare for that journey also. If we are faithful and keep the commandments of God, we will enter in through a gate that will lead to glorious wonders. *"Blessed are they that do his commandments, that they may have right to the tree of life, and may enter in through the gates into the city" (Revelation 22:14).*

The story does not end there. I was astonished at what had happened and how it had all happened so fast! For a few moments I felt disoriented and just stood there when suddenly another young man with my bags in tow came to me and said, "You are finished Madam, you may go, all of your things are there. It is finished!"

It is finished! Those are heavenly words also. In the future, the things of this world will be finished. God will come and take us on the journey of a lifetime. *"For the Lord Himself shall descend from heaven with a shout, with the voice of the archangel, and with the trump of God: and the dead in Christ shall rise first: Then we which are alive and remain shall be caught up together with them in the clouds, to meet the Lord in the air: and so shall we ever be with the Lord" (1 Thessalonians 4:16-17).* What a journey, the journey of a lifetime!

We will hear the words, "you may enter" again, if we are faithful. These words will be from our Blessed Redeemer. *"His lord said unto him, Well done, thou God and faithful servant: thou hast been faithful over a few things, I will make thee ruler over many things: enter thou into the joy of thy lord" (Mathew 25:21).* YOU MAY ENTER!

A Prayer for Today

Father, thank you for the joy of knowing that I will one day take the journey of a lifetime and will be with you forever. Amen.

Questions for Reflection, Prayer, and Meditation

1. Many people doubt their acceptance in Heaven because of past or current sins. Write a prayer for God to open up your heart to an understanding of His open door of love and grace which is His unmerited favor to you.

    _____

    _____

    _____

    _____

    _____

    _____

    _____

    _____

2. What does Revelation 22:14 say to you?

    _____

    _____

    _____

    _____

    _____

_____
_____
_____
_____
_____

3. God has a door available for you that is tremendous. Meditate on His unspeakable goodness and ability to open spiritual and physical doors in your life. What spiritual and physical doors do you need opened? Take a moment and talk to God about it right here and right now.

_____
_____
_____
_____
_____
_____
_____
_____
_____

YOUR RAY OF SONSHINE FOR TODAY

*Be open and ready
to walk through your door
of opportunity.*

DAY 25
A Powerful Name

Neither is there salvation in any other: for there is none other name under heaven given among men, whereby we must be saved.
Acts 4:12

And this is his commandment, That we should believe on the name of his Son Jesus Christ, and love one another, as he gave us commandment.
1 John3:22

When God calls your name, He does it with love, grace, mercy, and tenderness.
Janice J. Browne

God never mispronounces your name.
Janice J. Browne

My husband Benjamin and I were invited by a friend to attend a meeting where he would be the speaker and I would be the guest soloist. Our friend told us we would be staying at the mansion, but he did not prepare us for what our eyes would see. It was a mansion indeed! The house was just gorgeous and the grounds were magnificent. As far as the eyes could see, there was greenery, flowers and beauty everywhere. I could hardly wait until the next morning to jog. Morning came, Sweetie and I had our usual devotion together and off I went to jog. At the end of the first half of the jog, I decided to stop and take in the scenery. As I turned to look in one direction and then another, to my surprise stood a dog, a Pit Bull that did not seem very happy about my being there. What was I going to do? I was miles from the house. I quickly studied the situation and thought about what I should do. As the dog began to approach me with an angry growl, I cried out in the loudest voice I could, "Jesus! Jesus! Jesus! In my mind I remembered reading that demons flee at the name of Jesus. Surely, a dog ready to attack would also be stilled by that Name. I was defenseless, I was helpless, I was alone. The dog gradually came towards me, and each time I called the name of Jesus he stopped. How was this going to end?

There are times in this life when we feel defenseless, helpless, and danger lurks all around us. These dangers may be in situations, people or places, but we have a God who is ready to protect us. All we need to do is call upon His name. When we call, He hears us. God says to call upon His name and He will hear us (Zechariah 13:9).

His name is special; there is no other name like the name of Jesus. *"Wherefore God also hath highly exalted him, and given him a name which is above every name: That at the name of Jesus every knee should bow, of things in heaven, and things in earth, and things under the earth" (Philippians 2:9-10).* I can also say, at the name of Jesus that Pit Bull turned around and walked away. As the dog turned and walked away, I turned and jogged back to the house. All I could say was, "Thank you Jesus for saving me."

David says in Psalm 106:8, *"Nevertheless he saved them for his name's sake, that he might make his mighty power to be known."* I agree with David, when I called on His name for my protection from the dangerous attack of that Pit Bull, He saved me for His namesake and He made His mighty power to be known to me so that I could make it know to others." Right now, at this very moment, if you are in need of help, whatever it may be, just call on the name of Jesus. He will hear you and He will answer.

A Prayer for Today

Thank you, Jesus, for hearing me when I call on you. Your name is so precious and powerful. Amen.

Questions for Reflection, Prayer, and Meditation

1. Try to recall an instance when you were in physical or emotional danger and you called on the name of Jesus. What happened when you called?

   _____

   _____

   _____

   _____

   _____

   _____

   _____

   _____

2. Meditate and call on the name of Jesus for what you need at this very moment. He will hear you. Call Him now!

   _____

   _____

   _____

   _____

   _____

   _____

   _____

   _____

3. Sing a song that has the name of Jesus in it. Keep it in your heart and mind. Sing it when you need help or comfort. His name and the music will calm any situation that you encounter. It works!

_____

_____

_____

_____

_____

_____

_____

_____

_____

YOUR RAY OF SONSHINE FOR TODAY

*Call on His name
any time.*

DAY 26

Thank You for Befriending Me

Kindness is a form of love.
Janice J. Browne

God's love is unspeakable and cannot be superseded.
Janice J. Browne

My mom is a phenomenal mother and a tremendous woman of God. We talk often about her work as an Instructor of the Bible. She has told me many stories over the years. As a Bible Instructor for 42 years she had the opportunity to see thousands of people give their lives to Christ. The following story is one of my favorites, and I pray that you will be blessed as you read it.

As a backdrop to the story she was invited by a minister to be the Head Bible Instructor for an Evangelistic Crusade in Toronto, Canada. She arrived excited and ready to work for God. It was not very long before she was in the daily routine of praying, fasting, and visiting. Her duties included making face to face contact with the people whose names she received from a list that was compiled as they arrived each night.

This is how my mother tells the story: Interestingly, the person whose story I am sharing with you was not on a list, not my list or anyone else's on the staff. It seems he just simply came on his own to the meeting each night. I tried for weeks to get his address, but the young man said that he could not give me an address and no one else seemed to know him or where he lived.

I first saw and heard him on the back row of the massive auditorium, and as I looked at the young man a voice said to me, "Be kind and thoughtful to him." He was quite young, his appearance disheveled, his hair was matted, his clothes were dirty, and he left an unpleasant odor as he staggered to his seat each night. Some people were visibly uncomfortable with his presence. Each night I would warmly greet him and welcome him to the meetings.

As the young man continued to come nightly, the ushers and others who started to sit near him noticed that his attitude and language had changed. He no longer used foul language and moved from the back of the auditorium to a seat closer to the front.

After the first baptism, a clean cut, well-spoken young man came up to me and said, "Sister Johnson, you probably don't remember me, but I am the young man that you befriended. I am now a member of your church as a result of your being kind and thoughtful to me when I first came to these meetings. Thank you, Sister Johnson, for showing me Christ's love and kindness."

After attending the meetings nightly for six weeks, the young man made his decision to follow Christ all the way and to be baptized. I did not recognize the young man. I could hardly believe my eyes! A complete transformation had taken place in the young man's heart, life, and appearance.

I chose this story to show you the power of love and kindness. It was the simple act of love that drew the young man to Christ. We are reminded in the Bible that we are to love each other *"Beloved, let us love one another: for love is of God; and everyone that loveth is born of God, and knoweth God (1 John 4:7).*

A Prayer for Today

Father, help us to realize that the true gospel is God's love in action. Amen.

Questions for Reflection, Prayer, and Meditation

1. Have you ever extended kindness to someone that you would not ordinarily interact with? If so, how did you interact and what was the result?

   _____

   _____

   _____

   _____

   _____

   _____

   _____

   _____

   _____

2. Write some ways to show kindness to someone you do not currently interact with.

   _____

   _____

   _____

   _____

   _____

   _____

3. How has God been kind to you? Write a gratitude list below.

_____

_____

_____

_____

_____

_____

_____

_____

_____

_____

_____

YOUR RAY OF SONSHINE FOR TODAY

Befriend someone.

DAY 27
It's Never Too Late!

And I will restore to you the years that the locus hath eaten, the cankerworm, and the caterpiller, and the palmerworm, my great army which I sent among you. And ye shall eat in plenty, and be satisfied, and praise the name of the Lord your God, that hath dealt wondrously with you: and my people shall never be ashamed.
Joel 2:25-26

If any of you lack wisdom, let him ask of God, that giveth to all men liberally, and upbraideth not; and it shall be given him.
James 1:5

Late bloomers still bloom.
Janice J. Browne

Late bloomers outlast early bloomers.
Janice J. Browne

If you say it is too late, it will be too late. Your actions will follow your words.
Janice J. Browne

The first day of class is always interesting to me as I stand and watch students rush into the classroom to get the seat of their choice. Some walk in and sit confidently on the front row with enthusiastic anticipation while others jockey for a back seat in the corner. At any rate, watching this interaction gives me a good inner smile, and thoughts about what kind of students might be in the class.

On this particular first day of class in walked a petite little lady not more than five feet tall pulling an overstuffed book bag with a smile on her face and a glint in her eye. Her lovely smile and polite nod to me seemed to indicate she was pleasant and friendly. She had come into the classroom when most of the seats had been filled. She looked around and spotted a seat near the window midway the classroom.

The time came for us to begin the class. Each student sat with great expectancy as I introduced myself, described the course, and told them what I expected from them during the semester. I then asked each student to introduce themselves with one additional fact they wanted to share with the class.

The students were very interesting and shared wonderful information about themselves with the class. As the students shared their personal information they sat in their seats, but I noticed that when this student introduced herself she stood up with great dignity and said, "I am Merry, and I am looking forward to being with you this semester." She shared with us that she was excited about being back in school after being away for more than 50 years. The students gave her a big applause that warmed the room and her heart.

As time passed, I learned that she was 78 years old and had endured many hardships in her lifetime but was determined to obtain her degree. She was a diligent student whose work was impeccable. She soon became the darling of the class. If ever there was wit and intelligence combined, we had it in her.

From the beginning of the semester she never missed a class and was always prompt, however near the end of the semester I noticed that she had not attended class for two days consecutively and was tardy for three days. At the end of the next class I shared my concerns with her unusual absence and tardiness. I asked her if there was a problem or anything that I could do to help her. She apologized and assured me that she would not miss anymore classes and would be on time.

I later learned that Merry was carrying all her belongings in that overstuffed book bag that she had on the first day of class. She had been evicted from her small apartment because she could no longer pay the rent, she was homeless. After staying on the streets for a few days, the two days she missed class, she found a homeless shelter to live in, but there was no public transportation near the shelter, so she had to walk the distance of about eight miles on foot which caused her to be late for those three days.

I learned this information from a student who, saw Merry walking to class and offered her a ride for the rest of the semester. Merry was and is to me a phenomenal woman who could have given up her dream for education 50 years prior. At the end of the course we had a wonderful conversation. I learned so much from her, determination, endurance, grit, and a push-through-to-the-end attitude.

She told me she had been married to her husband for 40 years and that after his death it took a toll on her finances. Her only daughter that she lived with died and that further devastated her living conditions. With no one left and a small pension she decided that it was time to live her dream which was to go back to college and earn her degree.

She didn't talk about her plight with sadness but instead with excitement. These are the words she said to me at the end of the conversation "This is my next exciting chapter and I am going to finish it with success. Some people may think I am too old but it's never too late."

God helps us to succeed. He puts the dreams in our hearts. Sometimes, we get discouraged and negative events seem to block our desire to succeed. Darkness seems to cover our hearts and faces, but just as the Holy Spirit hovered over the face of the deep darkness when this world was created (Genesis 1:2) so it is that He hovers all around us and brings light, joy, determination, and hope to help us meet the tasks He sets before us. He is like the eagle who hovers over her eaglets in the nest. He teaches, strengthens, covers, and protects us while He helps us succeed. And then one day when we are ready to fly, to succeed, He pushes us out of the nest but flies beneath us to catch us if we fall.

"As an eagle stirreth up her nest, fluttereth, over her young, spreadeth abroad her wings,

taketh them, beareth them on her wings:" (Deuteronomy 32:11). And if we should fail at what we want to accomplish He will pick us up and teach us again. Keep trying, it's never too late.

Well, at the age of 78, Merry did succeed in my class and she's determined to complete her degree. After my conversation with Merry on the last day of class I packed up my books to leave, I noticed an envelope with my name on it in Merry's handwriting. I opened the enveloped and inside of it was a paper angel. On the back of the paper angel was the inscription "Angelic spirit of mercy and love, set my heart free to sore like a dove."

As I look at the little paper angel and read the words on the back of it my heart is deeply touched, and I pray that Merry will be set free to soar like a dove and that you to will be set free to soar like a dove, and be successful in your endeavors, because it's never too late!

A Prayer for Today

Father, thank you for giving me gifts and talents. Help me to use them starting today. Help me to stop procrastinating and complaining because it's never too late. Amen.

Questions for Reflection, Prayer, and Meditation

1. Read Matthew 7:7, Jeremiah 33:3 and apply the texts to your situation.

_____

_____

_____

_____

_____

_____

_____

_____

2. Read Deuteronomy 32:11 and write it down. You are the bird in that nest that God is protecting and teaching.

_____

_____

_____

_____

_____

_____

_____

_____

_____

3. List your dreams and write a prayer to fulfill them.

_____

_____

_____

_____

_____

_____

_____

_____

_____

YOUR RAY OF SONSHINE FOR TODAY

*It's not too late
for you to start
working on it today.*

DAY 28
A Tale of Two Tiny Messengers

Tiny messengers sometimes bring big messages.
Janice J. Browne

When we think God's gifts are small, in actuality, they are very big blessings.
Janice J. Browne

The stories that you are about to read are true, heartwarming, humorous, and awe inspiring. We can learn a lot from children. Even though we are parents, grandparents, teachers, cousins, aunts, and uncles, we can learn lessons from children. Yes! Children are leaders. We can learn from a little child, and sometimes, we need to follow them. After all, when we get to heaven a little child shall lead the animals.

Think about it, in a sinful world the animals and children would not be able to harmlessly be together. That kind of interaction would be harmful to the animals and the children. But the Bible reminds us that *"The wolf also shall dwell with the lamb, and the leopard shall lie down with the kid; and the calf and the young lion and the fatling together; and a little child shall lead them" (Isaiah 11:6).*

There are times adults act like animals toward each other by fighting and trying to destroy each other. If we look closely we can see children lead through their example. How many times have you fought with another person and held a grudge? Little children with argue and fight but they will forget and play with each other again as if it never happened.

It is humbling to forgive another especially if they have wronged you. There is greatness in humbleness. Children know how to forgive and move on. Children lead us to have that kind of attitude if we accept the lesson from them. The Bible account tells us, *"At the same time came the disciples unto Jesus, saying, Who is the greatest in the Kingdom of heaven? And Jesus called a little child unto Him, and set him in the midst of them, And said, Verily I say unto you, Except ye become converted, and become as little children, ye cannot enter into the kingdom of heaven"* (Matthew 18:1-3).

If heaven is our goal we must become as little children by being converted from anger, hurting others, backbiting and other destructive behaviors. We must become as little children. *"Whosoever therefore shall humble himself as this little child, the same is greatest in the kingdom of heaven"* (Matthew 18:4).

I am reminded of some beautiful words from my friend Charlotte Phillips, "Laugh when you can, apologize when you should, let go of what you can't change, life is too short to be anything but happy." Take note of why children are so happy. They will laugh without apology, don't carry grudges, and don't try to change others. What beautiful lessons from children!

Today I want to start the tale of two children with my sister, Cynthia Yvette. She was the sister born three years after me. I was so excited when my Mother and Father announced I would have a new little sister. Cynthia Yvette was my baby doll. She was clever, witty, and bright even as a little girl. I will never forget her ability to pick up everything around her like a little sponge. On Friday, my mother always prepared a special dinner with a delicious desert for the family.

Cynthia Yvette could not have been more than 3 years old. I shall never forget it was a lovely winter evening. My Mother had us all bathed, dressed and ready to meet our Dad when he came home from work. The house was sparkling clean, and dinner was all prepared. At the end of dinner, we would be served one of our Mother's special pies. Yummy! While we were eating dinner, the pie was baking. Periodically as we were eating dinner Mom, Dad or I would ask "Is the p-i-e ready yet?" Instead of saying the word "pie" we would spell it so that Cynthia Yvette would not know what it was and be surprised because pies were her favorite desert and my Mom wanted to surprise her. Dad would say "Do you think the P-i-e is baked yet?" I would ask Mom, "Do you think the p-i-e is ready?" To which she would reply with a smile and a twinkle in her eye "No, the p-i-e is not quite ready yet."

This question with the spelling of the word "pie" went on throughout dinner. We had such fun spelling and watching the look on Cynthia Yvette's face. She would quizzically look from person to person as we were spelling the word "pie." She would repeat the spelling to herself and look at us each time we asked the question about the pie.

Dinner ended, and Mother announced with a smile on her face that the "p-i-e" was ready. At this announcement Cynthia Yvette with the biggest smile and the most satisfied look on her face turned to my Mother and said, "Give me some of that p-i-e--pie!" She had learned that the letters p-i-e spelled her favorite desert, pie. We all laughed and realized that simply by listening to us, the little sponge had learned to spell a new word.

This reminds me that what we say and how we say it is being soaked into the mind of children as if they are little sponges. Children are very observant. They see what we do and hear what we say. It is our responsibility to be examples of God's love and grace. We are to teach them about Christ. *"And all thy children shall be taught of the Lord; and great shall be the peace of thy children"* (Isaiah 54:13). When they are taught about the love of Jesus, when turbulent times come, and the way is dark, peace will be their guide. Teach them!

The final tale in today's reading is the story of a little boy who is my nephew. Each year our family would attend a conference. At this conference we get to see a lot of our friends and hear wonderful music and presentations. At one such conference I had the joy of having my little nephew with me throughout the conference. He was so darling and articulate even at the age of four. I love to give my nieces and nephews gifts. Seeing the joy on their faces as they receive my gifts specially chosen for them is a reward for me.

On this occasion I gave my nephew a wrist watch. When I presented it to him he was so excited and proud of the wrist watch. The excitement and joy on his face was wonderful to observe. But it was not seeing the happiness on his face as he accepted the watch or his continuously looking at it as if he could read the time. The joy and the awe for me was when one of my friends greeted us, noticed the wrist watch and asked the question "Hey little buddy what time is it?" To which my nephew looked at his new wrist watch and with the sincerest facial expression replied "It's time for Jesus to come! Imagine a four-year-old saying that!

We could not believe our ears! Furthermore, we couldn't believe who the statement came from. How could he grasp such an event? It was obvious that his parents had followed the biblical principle of teaching him about Jesus and his return to this earth someday. That little sponge had soaked it up and without hesitation made the statement with total desire and anticipation!

Just think about it Jesus is coming personally to get us! Oh, to see Him face to face *"For the Lord himself shall descend from heaven with a shout, with the voice of the archangel, and with the trump of God: and the dead in Christ shall rise first: Then we which are alive and remain shall be caught up together with them in the clouds, to meet the Lord in the air: and so shall we ever be with the Lord"* (1 Thessalonians 4:16-17).

I can hardly wait for Jesus's return!

We can learn a lot from these two tiny messengers if we look, listen, and accept what God has shown us through them and will show us through other children. So, in closing this reading I ask the question of myself "What time is it?" My answer is the same as my little nephew, "Time for Jesus to come!

Let's be ready when He comes!

A Prayer for Today

Dear Father, help me to realize that my time on this earth is shorter than I think. Help me to be prepared and ready for the second coming of Christ Jesus. Amen.

Questions for Reflection, Prayer, and Meditation

1. God has given us children as special blessings. Write a prayer for children around the world who need to know God and how to

worship. Whether or not you have children, be an example of God's love to them and help them to be ready and joyfully waiting His return.

_____
_____
_____
_____
_____
_____
_____
_____
_____

2. Are you sharing with others the good news that Jesus is coming back to this earth to take us home to live with Him? What texts can you show them that He is returning to this earth? Read the text, write it out, and think on it for yourself also.

_____
_____
_____
_____
_____
_____
_____
_____
_____

3. Are you ready for Jesus to come? If not, how can you get ready?

_____
_____
_____
_____
_____
_____
_____

YOUR RAY OF SONSHINE FOR TODAY

*Become childlike today
and soak up God's love.*

DAY 29

Ellen

Angels are God's compassion compass.
Janice J. Browne

Be not forgetful to entertain strangers: for thereby some have entertained angels unawares.
Hebrews 13:1-3

Kindness shown is kindness received by God and us.
Janice J. Browne

There was a sea of faces that reflected excitement, anticipation, and curiosity. The music was beautiful. The hall was filled with students as far as the eye could see, and the expectation of having the American woman speaker added to the overall enthusiasm.

After all of the preliminaries and introduction I took my place at the podium with all eyes watching in total silence. Into the presentation I noticed heads moving in agreement, smiles and sometime peals of laughter. At one point the students were sitting on the edge of their seat and at the end, they all stood and applauded. I couldn't believe the response and felt so humbled that God had used me to speak to the students.

At the end of the program the other guests and I went to the door to shake hands only to notice that no one came. As I stood there I wondered if they had understood the presentation or if they were being polite when they stood and applauded. Just at the end of my questioning thoughts I felt a tiny hand slide into my hand and hold it firmly.

I looked down and right beside me holding my hand with her right hand and in her other hand a dirty worn little book with a picture of Jesus on it was a tiny very dirty little angel of a girl. She looked up at me with a big smile and squeezed my hand even tighter. As I looked down at this little figure my heart was moved and the only thing I could do was to reach down and give her a big hug.

Minutes later the Head Master rushed up to me and said "You are at the wrong door and hundreds of students are in line waiting to shake your hand. As we rushed to the other door the little girl never let go of my hand even as I was shaking the hands of the students.

A short time later we were invited to go to the luncheon that had been prepared for us. Of course, you know who went as my special guest, the little girl who continued to hold my hand. The servers were none too pleased that at the head table next to the other dignitaries, my husband and myself, sat a very dirty smelly little girl with matted hair, no shoes, a torn dress that was so dirty and faded that you couldn't figure out the color of it.

Even though she was offensive to the servers she was perfectly comfortable and so were my husband and I. Others at the table didn't seem to notice or look at her sitting at this long table, it was polite to honor the special guest and anyone she bought to the luncheon. I finally got an opportunity to ask her name only to find that she didn't understand my question because she and I spoke different languages. She didn't understand English and I didn't speak Amharic. Somehow, we managed to communicate despite our language barrier. In fact, there was no barrier between us and with much hand movement and smiles I found out that her name was Ellen.

At the end of dinner, a very kind woman noticed our interaction and makeshift conversation. The lady came to my rescue as translator. I found out that little Ellen live across the road from the school. Ellen came on the campus for the special celebrations and to church each week. Even though she sat in the children's class they did not sit near her nor communicate with her, I noticed that on another visit, but she didn't seem to be concerned. She listened and looked intently at the teacher.

I shared with my husband that I wanted to meet Ellen's mother because I knew this was the beginning of a wonderful friendship that God had sent to the both of us. He agreed, and I went with her and the kind lady across the road to meet Ellen's mother.

When we arrived, Ellen's mother met us with the most wonderful smile. She amazingly did speak a little English and greeted us with a warm "Hello, how are you?" The house was very small and dark with no windows or electricity. I understood the dirty condition of Ellen's clothing. She and her mother lived in a mud house with a dirt floor, walls, and a roof. My heart was saddened as I saw the condition of their home however, I thought about the many others on the street who didn't have a roof over their head.

After our greeting we introduced ourselves and invited her to come across the road for lunch with us to which she agreed. She told us she would come shortly, and she did with another little baby in her arms. We had a lovely lunch together and told her how we met Ellen. We asked if Ellen could visit with us at our home in Addis Ababa. She said yes immediately, and we agreed to send the driver to get her the following week. That would give us time to prepare for Ellen's visit with us.

The day arrived for Ellen's visit. We were very excited about our little guests' arrival. We had a yellow bedroom just for her and brand-new clothing. Sure, enough she arrived in her same attire and dirt all over her face and body. The first order of business was to get her a bath. I showed her the bath tub filled with bubbles, and with hand gestures told her to get into the water and that I would be just outside the door if she needed anything.

We could hear her splashing around in the water, laughing and giggling. Finally, I knocked on the door, peeked in and again with hand gestures told her it was time to end the bath. With much coaxing she reluctantly consented to get out of the bathtub.

When Ellen came out of the bathroom after spending almost an hour in the bathtub I couldn't believe my eyes! She was the most beautiful little girl I'd ever seen with big round Ethiopian eyes, a mass of curly hair and a big smile on her face! We both laughed together. After putting on one of her chosen dresses we presented her to my husband and the reaction was the same, a big smile and disbelief!

We enjoyed Ellen's frequent visits with us. She brought so much, fun, life and girly mischief to our home. She sang one song in English over and over again even when she was making a request. The song was "Twinkle, twinkle little star…" I can still hear her voice and see her face as she sang with gusto and right on key.

We love Ellen until this very day and consider her our little angel. My husband and I helped Ellen and her mother. We were able to completely renovate their house from mud to more permanent material with the help of a dear friend who was the overseer of the project for us. We made it clear that included in the renovation was electricity and a personal wash area so that Ellen's mother would not need to wash in the river behind the house.

When we left Ethiopia the house renovation was still in progress and one day we received pictures of the completed project and I shall never forget one of the phrases in the letter by Ellen's mother, it said, "Thank you, my house is like heaven on earth!"

This story reminds me of God and us. We put our dirty hands into his pure, holy, nail-print hands and He holds them with tender love and care. If He takes care of the flowers how much more will He take care of us? He feeds us each day with food, clothes and He shelters us. We don't have to *worry* *"But even the very hairs of your head are all numbered. Fear not therefore: ye are of more value than many sparrows" (Luke 12: 7).*

We are filthy with the dirt of sin all over us, but if we confess our sins He cleanses us from them. *"If we confess our sins, he is faithful and just to forgive us our sins, and to cleanse us from all unrighteousness" (1 John 1: 9).*

He also feeds us spiritually with His Word daily. You are reading His words today. Our name may or may not be Ellen, God knows your name-He has engraved it on the palm of His hand and holds us with His hand *"Behold, I have graven thee upon the palms of my hand; they walls are continually before me"* (Isaiah 49:16). All we need to do is hold on and never let go. Still, if you do, He will always stretch His hands out to you.

One final thought. Ellen's mother said her newly renovated house was like heaven on earth. One day we will have a new eternal home and a newly renovated house-our bodies. If you are sick today remember, *"For we know that if our earthly house of this tabernacle were dissolved, we have a building of God, a house not made with hands, eternal in heavens."* (2 Corinthians 5:1) Oh what unspeakable joy! Let God hold you and He will keep you today and always.

A Prayer for Today

Dearest Father, I thank you for teaching me about your love through the little angel, Ellen. Thank you for cleaning me up to my full beauty in you. Amen.

Questions for Reflection, Prayer, and Meditation

1. Has God ever sent an angel in disguise for you to show kindness? If so who, when and where?

   _____

   _____

   _____

   _____

   _____

   _____

   _____

   _____

   _____

2. How has God held your hand and under what circumstances?

_____
_____
_____
_____
_____
_____
_____
_____
_____

3. You don't have to renovate someone's house just do some small deed for someone this week. Make a call, send a card, or visit a person who needs your kindness. Write their name and the plan below.

_____
_____
_____
_____
_____
_____
_____
_____
_____

YOUR RAY OF SONSHINE FOR TODAY

Be kind today.
There is nothing in the world
that compares to
doing something good
for someone else!

DAY 30

The Piano

Every good gift and every perfect gift is from above, and cometh down from the Father of Lights, with whom is no variableness, neither shadow of turning.
James 1:17

A gift from the heart is timeless.
Janice J. Browne

Real love is a gift that lasts forever.
Janice J. Browne

Gifts are wonderful! The very sound and thought of the word "gift" evokes feelings of delight and happiness. Gifts are interesting in that they may be from the heart or they may be given because it is a tradition for a holiday or a special occasion. Gifts make us laugh, smile, cry, and in some cases, give us as much or more joy than the receiver of the gift. Their thrill just absolutely flows from their heart to ours.

Sometimes gifts are expected and at other times they may come as a complete surprise. I have been the recipient of both expected and surprise gifts. But I think this is one of my hall of fame surprise gifts. I was talking on the telephone to a friend about some music would we would perform together. She would be my accompanist for a solo that I was requested to sing. As we talked about the arrangement of the song we decided on the time and day we needed to rehearse. In the course of the conversation, we decided that the location of the rehearsal would be at her home because she had a piano.

The night before the conversation with my friend I had just told God before I fell off to sleep that it was okay for me not to have the piano that I had been asking for in prayer and planning to purchase. The timing was never right and the one I wanted would cost a small fortune. Without sadness, anger, bitterness, or any negative feelings with a sweet prayerful attitude I simply said God it's okay not to get the piano.

Let me go back to the prior conversation with my friend which took place the next day after my resolve of not needing a piano. As we were about to hang up I thanked her for the beautiful gift of playing the piano and willingness to minister with me then simply said I wish I had a piano then we could practice at my house to which she replied without hesitation, "You can have mine."

I didn't believe what I thought I heard her say. I politely said "What did you just say about your piano? She said "I am moving from my house and where I am going there won't be enough room for the piano, and I don't want to sell it nor put it in storage. I have been praying to give it to someone who would appreciate and take care of the piano. You are the person who I want to have the piano.

I couldn't believe what she was saying. I had just told God the night before that it was okay and that I was fine without a piano. Here she was saying, I prayed, and you are the one to have the piano. I told her that I could not accept such a gift and would keep it for her should she ever want it back to which she replied with a smile and a twinkle in her eye, "Okay. But it is yours."

What a gift! Such an unselfish act of kindness! A gift that was unbelievable to me. I couldn't imagine she would give me something so precious and cherished. This story reminds me of another unselfish, unspeakable gift of love. *"For God so loved the world, that He gave His only begotten Son, that whosoever believeth in Him should not perish, but have everlasting life (John 3:16).* It brings tears to my eyes as I think about how The Father would give His precious

152

cherished only son to die for me and that His only son would give up His life. An unbelievable gift! What a timeless eternal gift of love. Thank you, Father, and thank you Jesus for love that I cannot fathom!

A Prayer for Today

Loving Father, thank you for your unspeakable gift of love, the death of your only Son just for us. Amen.

Questions for Reflection, Prayer, and Meditation

1. Have you ever given someone a precious or cherished gift? How did it make you and the other person feel?

   _____

   _____

   _____

   _____

   _____

   _____

   _____

   _____

   _____

2. God the Father has given us the precious gift of His one and only cherished Son. What does that say to you? Receive your cherished gift at this moment.

   _____

   _____

   _____

   _____

   _____

   _____

   _____

   _____

   _____

3. Have you accepted the gift of Jesus? If so write a thank you prayer and if not, it is not too late. Just write the words "I accept you dear Jesus into my life at this very moment."

_____

_____

_____

_____

_____

_____

_____

_____

_____

YOUR RAY OF SONSHINE FOR TODAY

*Jesus is
your eternal
timeless gift of love.*

DAY 31

My Real Father

And will be a Father unto you, and ye shall be my sons and daughters, saith the Lord Almighty.
2 Corinthians 6:17

Some of the greatest qualities of a loving father are being dependable, trustworthy, and loving you unconditionally.
Janice J. Browne

To have a Father who is there for you, who believes in you, and trumpets everything you strive to do as greatness is the best kind of father.
Janice J. Browne

For some people when they hear the word Father it strikes terror, hurt, anger, and sometimes memories of physical and emotional pain. For others, as is my case, the word "father" evokes memories of pure love, joy, protection, and happiness. Wise, caring, encouraging, motivator, responsible, and most of all, Christian, are a few words that describe a wonderful father. My father was all of that and more.

One day as I watched a popular television personality host a program that focused on fathers missing from the lives of their children and the long-lasting effects it had on the children, fathers, family members and other relationships, it started me thinking about my own father. As I listened to a program with story after story about the devastation of an absent father, loneliness, bitterness, and self-doubt, I felt it necessary to give those of you who read this a view of the other side. I want to share what it is like to have a positively present father in your life.

He didn't accidently become a good father. He followed in the footsteps of his own father. He followed his father's faith, employment, and took care of the family just as his father had. He loved and admired his father with all of his heart.

I remember my father telling me about hearing his father's last breath as he slowly left this earth. What pain, what sorrow. His hero was gone! But he was the embodiment of his upstanding, outstanding father who was loved and respected in the community.

My father was the second eldest of six children and after the death of his father my father while his eldest brother attended school took on the responsibility of being the head of the family. He worked where his father worked, took care of his siblings and mother just as his father had done.

One day he met and married a beautiful young woman who was to be my mother. He told her he desired to have six children like his parents. She consented. Whew! What a woman! She agreed to his request! He was an outstanding husband and father who worked diligently, always came home, and took very good care of us. My mother was an outstanding wife and homemaker who had given up her career in nursing to be a stay-at-home mom. When we were older, and she was ready for a second career she became a Bible Instructor. That career took her around the world. He was very godly proud of her and encouraged her throughout her outstanding international 42-year career.

My father had an interesting way of dealing with us. We all realized he was a loving father because we saw the sacrifices he made for us. He would even forego looking at sports on television so that we could look at some girly show. That may seem small but try asking a man to do that today and it may be a small problem especially if there is only one television!

He was always interested in our days after a long day on his own job. He was an avid reader of the newspaper, kept up with the daily news and could be seen morning and evening reading his Bible. He loved books and I can imagine that this book would have been one of his favorites on his list of best loved books. I still have his library card to this day.

My parents were a wonderful Christian team who worked together to teach and cultivate us into good Christians and citizens. They always had evening worship with us. We all took part, singing, reciting the Bible, or telling a Bible story. It was like a live program with each of us taking turns being the Master of Ceremony. What a fun way to worship. My parents were very creative.

Father and Mother worked diligently to educate all six children from Christian elementary school all the way through graduate studies for the master's degrees. It was a tradition that upon completion of each degree, we would have a private family celebration and present the diploma to our parents. They beamed with joy and happiness at our accomplishments.

As I think back in time my father did something that to this day stands out in my mind. Whatever he thought he saw in us as a profession would be the name he would call us. As an example, he would refer to my younger brother as "Preacher" and sure enough he became a preacher. He referred to one of my sister's as "Editor" and years later she studied journalism and became an editor. The name he had for me was Professor. Can you guess what I became? You are correct I became a Professor in the field of Psychology. Each of us acquired professional names and became those professionals, all six of us!

One day my father was diagnosed with Mesothelioma cancer of the lungs. Forty years of working in a steel mill had taken its toll on his lungs. My world came crashing down. How could this be? Others worked there, and they didn't become ill. How could such a good man receive a death sentence? How could God let a man who other young men looked up to who had no father die? He mentored them as though they were his own sons.

I, along with my mother and siblings, took care of my father. Just as he heard his father's last breath, I heard his last breath. The pain and agony were and still is indescribable. I just couldn't believe God allowed this to happen. I loved and admired my father just as he did his father with all of my heart.

After his transition from this world we celebrated with deep sorrow and sadness the life of a "Fallen Prince" with hundreds of family, friends, and supporters. He was truly a "Prince of a Man" who had a humble royalty about him. Now I know that it was because he came from royal patronage the royal family of heaven.

His real father is King of the universe not the father he loved who we later found out was himself an orphan. How he became such a great father to my father with no example to follow as he raised himself tells me that he was also of royal patronage.

The end had come for my father and it was now time for me to join my husband in Ethiopia where we had been called to mission service. My Dad always took me wherever I went on the first day. He went with me on the first day of elementary school, college, and graduate school but he was not there for this occasion. I remember my mother telling me had my father been alive they together would have taken me to my husband but since he was no longer with us she would take me. She took me and stayed three months with us to be sure that I settled in and was okay.

This is really where the story begins about my real father. One day after my mother was gone back to the United States and my husband had traveled to another town in Ethiopia, it all came crashing down on me. I wept inconsolably. I cried from the deepest well of tears. I sobbed like I had never ever sobbed before. I couldn't stop crying, each time I tried it became worse, and I thought I would never stop. My pain and sorrow were so heavy that I felt as if I would suffocate from the weight of it.

It was then that I screamed out loud to God "How could you take such a good man? How could you take my father from me? How could you take my Dad? He was my father! When I heard myself crying and talking to God that way I became frightened and afraid. How dare I talk to God in that way? I continued to say other and over "My father is gone!" I began to apologize to God and tell Him that I was so sorry to ask Him those questions.

I didn't want God to think I loved my Dad more than Him. I felt awful and afraid that He might even think that I was worshipping my father over him. I wasn't worshipping him; I just missed my Dad so much and couldn't bear the thought of someone who loved me so much no longer being with me. Our long talks about absolutely anything at any time had come to an end.

As surely as you are reading this story a warm and loving voice said to me, "You don't need to apologize. I understand how much you loved him. I understand your grief and pain. I am not jealous of that love that you had for him. It is okay. I gave him to you. I am glad that you loved my gift to you of your earthly father so much." I couldn't believe my ears! And then He said these words to me "you are not alone. Yes, your earthly father is gone but I, your heavenly Father, am still here with you."

That is when I met my real father.

You may or may not have a father like mine. If you do and he is still with you, remember to celebrate him and spend as much time as you can with him. If you don't know your father let me introduce you to your real Father. He says to you that He will never leave you nor forsake you. He says to you, *"Lo, I am with you always, even unto the end of the world. Amen" (Matthew 28:20).*

He will comfort you in all of your pain, grief, and troubles. His wonderful words to you are, *"I will not leave you comfortless: I will come to you" (John 14:18).* He is so loving and wants you *to "Cast all your cares upon him; for he careth for you" (1 Peter 5:7).*

You can talk to him in prayer at anytime and anywhere. He will hear you. Let me leave you with a prayer to our real Father with the joy that someday we will be with Him forever.

After this manner therefore pray ye:
Our Father which art in heaven, Hallowed be thy name.
Thy kingdom come, Thy will be done in earth, as it is in heaven.
Give us this day our daily bread. And forgive us our debts, as we forgive our debtors. And
lead us not into temptation, but deliver us from evil: For thine is the kingdom, and the
power, and the glory, forever. Amen. **Matthew 6:9-13**

A Prayer for Today

Dear Father, thank you for being my real father. Thank you for loving and caring for me. I take comfort in knowing that you are with me and will always be with me. Amen.

Questions for Reflection, Prayer, and Meditation

1. If you know and have had a positive relationship with your earthly father, write down the wonderful things that you remember about him and include a prayer of thanksgiving.

   _____

   _____

   _____

   _____

   _____

   _____

   _____

   _____

   _____

2. If you do not know your father and feel emptiness or bitterness in your heart, write a prayer to God about your concern.

   _____

   _____

   _____

   _____

   _____

   _____

   _____

   _____

   _____

   _____

3. If your father is deceased and you did not have a positive relationship with him, ask God for the strength to forgive your father. Write that request to God below. If you also choose to do so, you may write your deceased father a letter telling him your hurts, and after talking with God for strength, forgive your father and burn the letter. It is over you are free to forgive and to love.

_____

_____

_____

_____

_____

_____

_____

_____

_____

YOUR RAY OF SONSHINE FOR TODAY

Your real Father
loves you
with all of His heart.

161

A Concluding Blessing

"May you bask in the SONshine of God's love as it flows over you each day. May He place a crown of wisdom upon your head and set you upon a throne of greatness for His sake."

-Janice J. Browne

Dearest Friend,

We have come to the end of our 31 days of SONshine for the Mind, Soul, Body, and Spirit journey. I hope and pray that you were blessed by each story.

There were times I cried, not just because of sadness but because of the beautiful reminders of how much I am loved and cared for by my real Father-God. You, and I, are loved beyond words and cared for by the mercy and grace of our real Father-God.

At other times, I laughed out loud as the fond memories of so many humorous events flooded my mind. Think of your own humorous events and remember to laugh out loud!

I hope that if we should meet on this earth face-to-face or through technology, at your book club, a book signing, or by God's design just passing on the street I'd love to share with you pictures of our lovely dog "Mr. Browne," the white sofa, and the pear tree.

I pray that we can share many more 31 Days of SONshine together for many years to come. If we do not meet on this earth I look forward to seeing you in heaven. I extend an invitation to meet you for lunch on the right side of the Tree of Life (see Revelation 2:7).

Sincerely,

Dr. Janice J. Browne

Acknowledgements

I am most appreciative to *God the Father, Son and Holy Spirit* for creating the setting for each story and bringing this book to fruition.

Special thanks posthumously to *William "Bill" Cleveland* my friend and first editor of a portion of the stories. Bill graciously treated each story with delicate care and understanding. I await our reunion that we spoke of in the story "Hats and Crowns" … see you there.

Thank you, *Penny Wheeler,* for editing a second portion of the stories with the thought in mind that the creation (my writing) is an idea to be kept intact and for respecting my voice as the writer.

Benjamin my sweet husband, thank you for your patience and for reading the manuscript over and over again and offering helpful suggestions that made it the book it is today.

I am forever grateful to you, *Mother,* for your love, for believing in me, for pushing me daily to finish what I started and for your support in every way. I humbly thank you.

An immense thank you to my remaining sisters, *Stephanie* for your love and positive encouragement, and *Rosalind* for your love, invaluable encouragement and editorial insights. You are both priceless!

To my remaining brother, *Washington II,* a writer's writer, you totally inspire me! For your editorial assistance and powerful suggestions, I am sincerely thankful.

To *Kemi* my niece-daughter for your encouragement, helpful suggestions, and insightful comments. You are my precious sunshine.

Sincere gratitude to my cousin-brother, encourager and supporter, *Robert "Bobby" Johnson,* for writing such a rich and engaging Foreword. Your words overflow with grace, inspiration and ethos.

Heartfelt gratitude to my God-sister, *Paula Blackwell,* who is my catalyst, encourager, supporter, go-to girl for everything! You are the best! Thank you for connecting me to Athena C. Shack, a true professional, woman of God and fulfiller of dreams.

Thank you, *Ellie Wharton* you are an elegant writer and my encouraging friend to the end.

Dr. Gazetta Holt-Roberts thank you for your editorial insights, and *Dr. Danny Blanchard* for your monumental encouragement.

A tremendous thank you to *Lucas and Alicia Johnson* for your keen insights, proof reading and helpful editorial suggestions.

Grateful appreciation to the participants in each story. You have positively and spiritually enriched my life.

Prayer is the key to the writing and completion of this book. Thank you to all of my *Prayer Warriors* who, P-U-S-H-E-D - prayed until something happened.

Thank you to *Karen Black, Terrence Brown, Monique Elliot,* and *Marion Fowler* for your daily prayers; *Clementine Maria Collins* and your awesome prayer group "Light My Path Ministries" for fasting and praying each Tuesday for two years; my consistent Facebook Prayer Warriors and to countless others who pray for me 24/7 around the world.

Abundant gratitude to Athena C. Shack owner/publisher of Watersprings Media House and team for your patience, persistence, and professionalism that skillfully brought my words and dreams to life. God be praised!

For those whose names are not mentioned, it is not intentional— you know who you are. Continue to pray for me as I pray for you.

Last but certainly not least, thank you *Cynthia and Grayland* for being the voice in my head encouraging me to write and publish this book.

Meet the Author

First and foremost, Janice Johnson Browne is a prayer warrior who not only prays for her family and friends but for others whom she has never met in person.

Browne is an international speaker, educator, seminar presenter, consultant, personal growth developer, visionary, life coach and trainer. She is a General Civil Mediator approved by the Supreme Court of Tennessee and a master storyteller.

She holds a Bachelor of Science degree in Psychology is from Oakwood University, a Master of Science in Clinical Psychology from Alabama A& M University and earned her Doctor of Philosophy degree in Leadership from Andrews University. She was presented with an Honorary Doctor of Humane Letters from Daniel Payne College for her numerous and outstanding contributions to humanity.

Dr. Browne has been a university educator in the field of psychology for more than 20 years. Her passion is growing the mind, soul, and spirit of every individual she meets through consulting, counseling, speaking, training, in her classroom or in a conversation at the grocery store.

She is a dynamic, passionate, inspirational speaker and has traveled the world with life changing results as indicated by the numerous messages and e-mails she receives daily.

She is a student of all cultures and peoples of the world. Dr. Janice and her husband, Pastor Benjamin Browne were missionaries in Ethiopia for four years. He served as the President of the Ethiopia Union Mission and she worked as Special Assistant to the Deputy Director at the United States Agency for International Development (USAID) and as a Senior Associate Professor of Psychology at Addis Ababa University.

Her life experiences have empowered her to be a richly colorful storyteller who draws the listener in while educating and inspiring them with compassion, hope, and encouragement. Dr. Janice believes everyone has a story to share. She is the co-author of Gifts of Hope: Stories for Women by Women and of a spoken word CD SONshine for the Mind, Soul, Body, and Spirit.

She has appeared on television and radio programs including the Hope Channel, Birmingham Public Television, 3ABN Television and 3ABN Radio to name a few.

Dr. Browne is a life-coach and sought-after expert for offering her sagacious thoughts on life-quality, personal and professional leadership, relationships, cultural diversity, and organizational and management skills. She has been the speaker, presenter and trainer for thousands of women, parents, mental health organizations, youth conferences, and educational, church, and corporate institutions internationally. She considers herself a citizen of the world, a student of life, and a messenger of hope and encouragement.

Dr. Janice conducts prayer sessions for prayer conferences, delivers keynote addresses and seminars for women's organizations, corporations, parent-teacher groups, and professional conferences, and associations. Some of her clients have included Bryce Hospital, the University of Alabama, Loma Linda University, Tennessee Commission on Children and Youth, Southwest Union, and South Central Conference.

She has been blessed to share her gifts on 6 continents and in 30 countries that include Canada, Malawi, Ethiopia, China, Thailand, Philippines, Zimbabwe, Nigeria and Ukraine Women's Ministries Conferences, and others.

Browne was privileged to be an invited presenter by the General Conference of Seventh-day Adventist Women's Ministry Department on the subject "Forgiveness and Your Health," for a worldwide Health and Lifestyle Conference in Geneva, Switzerland.

Dr. Browne is a gifted musician whose lyric soprano voice has been compared to that of an angel on earth. Her musical treatment and dramatic presentation of hymns, contemporary, spiritual, and classical renditions are extraordinary. She has been blessed to share her God-given gift around the world and is available to share it with anyone who loves the gift of song.

If you are looking for tailor-made keynote address, presentations, seminars specific to your needs presented with tenacity, professionalism, enthusiasm, and knowledge, Dr. Janice J. Browne is available.

Your Thoughts

If you have been encouraged, inspired, renewed, and refreshed by participating in the 31 Days of SONshine experience, feel free to email me your thoughts

Prayer is the driving force in the 31 Days of SONshine Book Series. Each book has been prayed over. I am praying for you and I request that you pray for me. If you have a special prayer need, email your prayer requests to the prayer request portal on my website.

Do you have a true inspirational story you want published that fits the spirit of 31 Days of SONshine? I am planning future editions using a similar format that will feature true stories of love, lessons learned, triumphs, humor, hope, inspiration, and encouragement. I am looking for stories that captivate, motivate, and bring healing to the mind, soul, body, and spirit. The stories can be up to 1200 words and should be edited.

I am personally inviting you to join in future 31 Days of SONshine projects for consideration of your special story. If your story is considered for publication. You will be credited as one of the authors and have a biographical paragraph included in the book. For further inquiries you may contact me at janicejbrowne25@gmail.com

A portion of the proceeds from the sale of this book will go to the Brothers of Charity located in Addis Ababa, Ethiopia.

Connect with Author

For further information about books, CDs or to schedule a presentation you may contact:

Dr. Janice J. Browne
P.O. Box 158
Whites Creek, Tennessee 37189

 Janice Johnson Browne

 @janicejohnsonbrowne

 janicebrowne25@gmail.com

 www.drjanicebrownetoday.com

Made in the USA
Lexington, KY
22 November 2019